Biographical Supplement and Index

THE YOUNG OXFORD HISTORY OF
AFRICAN AMERICANS

Robin D. G. Kelley and Earl Lewis
General Editors

Biographical Supplement and Index

❖ ❖ ❖

David M. P. Freund

Marya Annette McQuirter

Oxford University Press
New York • Oxford

For Janine, Andrew, Amelia, and Gabrielle
—D.M.P.F.
For Raneesha and Taylor
—M.A.M.

Oxford University Press

Oxford   New York
Athens Auckland Bangkok Bogotá Bombay
Buenos Aires Calcutta Cape Town Dar es Salaam Delhi
Florence Hong Kong Istanbul Karachi
Kuala Lumpur Madras Madrid Melbourne
Mexico City Nairobi Paris Singapore
Taipei Tokyo Toronto
and associated companies in
Berlin   Ibadan

Biographical Supplement copyright © 1997 by David M. P. Freund and Marya Annette McQuirter
Museums and Historic Sites and Series Index copyright © 1997 by Oxford University Press, Inc.

Published by Oxford University Press, Inc.,
198 Madison Avenue, New York, New York 10016

Oxford is a registered trademark of Oxford University Press

Listing of Museums and Historic Sites compiled by Michelle Gates Moresi
Design: Sandy Kaufman and Leonard Levitsky

Library of Congress Cataloging-in-Publication Data
Freund, David M. P.
Biographical Supplement and Index / David M. P. Freund and Marya Annette McQuirter
p. cm. — (Young Oxford history of African Americans: v. 11)
Includes index.
ISBN 0-19-510258-4 (library ed.); ISBN 0-19-508502-7 (series, library ed.)
1. Afro-Americans—Biography—Dictionaries—Juvenile literature.
2. Historic sites—United States—Guidebooks—Juvenile literature.
3. Young Oxford history of African Americans—Indexes.
4. Afro-Americans—History—Juvenile literature—Indexes.
5. Blacks—America—History—Juvenile literature—Indexes.
I. McQuirter, Marya A. II. Title. III. Series.
E185.Y68   1995 vol. 11
[E185.96]
920'.009296073—dc21
96-54619
CIP

1 3 5 7 9 8 6 4 2

Printed in the United States of America
on acid-free paper

On the cover: *Clockwise from top left: Harriet Tubman, Frederick Douglass,*
Mary McLeod Bethune, and W. E. B. Du Bois
Frontispiece: *Emancipation Day parade, Richmond, Virginia, 1905*

CONTENTS

◇ ◇ ◇

A NOTE FROM THE AUTHORS

This volume profiles a selection of the people who appear in volumes 1 through 10 of The Young Oxford History of African Americans. *In this book we take a closer look at the backgrounds, experiences, and contributions of individuals who were involved in a wide range of activities and professions. We hope that these biographies encourage readers to further investigate the lives of these and other African Americans.*

THE YOUNG OXFORD HISTORY OF
AFRICAN AMERICANS

A company of black recruits at the naval training station in Great Lakes, Illinois, August, 1943.

Biographical Supplement

Abbott, Robert Sengstacke

NEWSPAPER EDITOR, PUBLISHER

Born: November 24, 1870
Frederica, St. Simon's Island, Georgia

Died:. February 29, 1940
Chicago, Illinois

Robert Abbott, founder of the *Chicago Defender* newspaper, created the first black newspaper of the 20th century that sought the masses for its readership base, laying the foundation for the development of the modern black press. Abbott kept his readers informed about local, national, and international news and used his publication to protest racism and segregation.

Abbott spent most of his youth in the South. He attended Beach Institute in Savannah, Georgia, and Claflin University in Orangeburg, South Carolina. At Hampton Institute in Virginia he studied printing from 1892 to 1896. He traveled west to Chicago to earn a law degree at Kent College of Law.

After receiving his degree in 1898, he left Chicago for five years to practice law in Indiana and Kansas.

Abbott founded the *Chicago Defender* in 1905. At its inception, he served as editor, writer, and business manager (Abbott could be seen selling newspapers on the streets of Chicago). Neighborhood institutions such as beauty parlors, barbershops, churches, and poolrooms also served as drop-off points. They increased the circulation of the newspaper and provided Abbott with news items for the next issues.

The Great Migration of blacks into the urban North and West during and after World War I turned the fledgling one-man operation into a successful newspaper company. Although Abbott did not initially support the migration from the rural South to the urban North and West, his paper eventually became an important source of news. Abbott paid railroad porters to deliver the papers to hired agents in the South who distributed the newspapers, often at great risk. (White landowners did not want their workers migrating to the North.) Rural and urban Southerners wrote hundreds of letters to the *Defender* seeking information about housing, employment, education, and financial support for their journey.

For Abbott the *Defender* provided a means to express his political views—particularly about African Americans agitating for their civil rights. Quotes such as "If you must die, take at least one with you" and "An eye for an eye" were imprinted boldly in the newspaper. Articles about the bombings of black homes in predominantly white neighborhoods, lynchings, and race riots were meant to keep African Americans informed but also impel them to action. The *Defender* also provided Abbott a forum to criticize black leaders whose ideas he disagreed with. By fostering a reading public, Abbott contributed to the development of a national black community.

FURTHER READING
Ottley, Roi. *The Lonely Warrior: The Life and Times of Robert S. Abbott*. Chicago: H. Regnery, 1955.

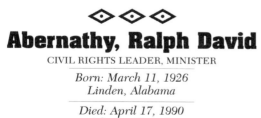

Abernathy, Ralph David

CIVIL RIGHTS LEADER, MINISTER

Born: March 11, 1926
Linden, Alabama

Died: April 17, 1990
Atlanta, Georgia

"My pulpit is wherever suffering and misery are." This was one of Ralph Abernathy's favorite sayings. He was a close friend and political colleague of Martin Luther King, Jr., and the two were often called the "civil rights twins." Abernathy was one of the principal leaders of the Montgomery bus boycott, helped to found the Southern Christian Leadership Conference (SCLC), and continued the Poor People's Campaign that SCLC had initiated before the assassination of King in 1968.

Abernathy was born into a large family on a farm owned by his parents. He was able to avoid farm work, spending most of his time reading, writing, and teaching Sunday school. Abernathy received his undergraduate degree from Alabama State College (now Alabama State University) in 1950. A year later he received his M.A. in sociology from Atlanta University. After his graduation, he returned to Alabama State, serving as dean of men and as a sociology instructor.

One of Abernathy's religious and political mentors was Vernon Johns, pastor of the Dexter Avenue Baptist Church in Montgomery, Alabama, and an outspoken critic of segregation in Alabama. He met Johns when Abernathy became pastor of the First Baptist Church, the oldest black church in Montgomery, in 1951.

Following the success of the year-long activism of the Montgomery bus boycott, Abernathy met with other ministers in Atlanta and formed the Southern Christian Leadership Conference in 1957. Abernathy was elected secretary-treasurer. Amidst the excitement of this new organization, Abernathy received a phone call from his pregnant wife, who informed him that their house had been bombed. He found out later that the First Baptist Church had also been bombed.

Abernathy succeeded King as president of SCLC after King's death in 1968. Six weeks after King's assassination, Abernathy led the Poor People's Campaign (PPC) to Washington, D.C. The PPC was founded to call attention to the extreme poverty that existed throughout the United States. The campaign was doused, however, by continuous rain, among other problems. Further, Abernathy was criticized for choosing to stay in a hotel instead of in Resurrection City, where as many as 2,500 people lived and protested on the Mall. The campaign was somewhat redeemed by the success of Solidarity Day on June 19, which drew more than 50,000 people. In his speech that day, Abernathy emphasized economic justice and the importance of anti-racist efforts. The following year, Abernathy and SCLC supported the striking workers of Local 1199B of the National Hospital and Nursing Home Employees Union in Charleston, South Carolina, who sought union recognition, higher pay, and better working conditions.

After Abernathy resigned from SCLC, he ran unsuccessfully in 1978 for the Democratic nomination to the House of Representatives. In 1980, he and longtime activist Hosea Williams served as co-organizers of Black Leaders Supporting President-elect Ronald Reagan.

PUBLICATION
And the Walls Came Tumbling Down: An Autobiography (1989)

FURTHER READING
Branch, Taylor. *Parting the Waters: America in the King Years, 1954–1963.* New York: Simon & Schuster, 1988.
Williams, Juan. *Eyes on the Prize: America's Civil Rights Year: 1954–1965.* New York: Penguin, 1988.

◆ ◆ ◆

Ali, Muhammad (Cassius Marcellus Clay, Jr.)

BOXER, ACTIVIST

*Born: January 17, 1942
Louisville, Kentucky*

Muhammad Ali (born Cassius Marcellus Clay, Jr.) began competitive fighting at age 12, just months after an instructor at a community recreation center in Louisville invited him to join a boxing class. Training six days a week as a teenager, he won virtually all of his 108 amateur bouts, two National Golden Glove Championships, and two National Amateur Athletic Union championships. In 1960, when he was 18, Clay won a gold medal in the light heavyweight division at the Olympics. That fall he turned pro and continued to amaze the boxing world with his quickness, his remarkable skills, and his bobbing, dancing style of fighting. After 19 professional victories, Clay won the world heavyweight crown in 1964 with a technical knockout of Sonny Liston. Clay successfully defended the title for three years.

Soon after the first title bout, Clay's life outside the ring took center stage when he publicly stated that he had renounced Christianity and joined the Nation of Islam. Explaining that Cassius Clay was his "slave" name, he changed it to Muhammad Ali. While Ali's membership in the Nation of Islam brought even more respect to the movement in the eyes of many blacks, most whites saw the Nation as an anti-white and anti-

American hate group, and thus treated Ali with hostility.

Ali was drafted into the armed forces in April 1967 but refused to report for induction, citing his religious opposition to joining the military. The World Boxing Association immediately stripped him of his title and his boxing license, and a Texas court sentenced him to a five-year prison sentence. After three and a half years of appeals, the U.S. Supreme Court reversed the conviction, and the NAACP forced the federal courts to order the renewal of his boxing license. Ali could not fight for a living during these years, but his courageous public defiance in the name of religious and political principles inspired black people throughout the world and helped energize the civil rights and peace movements in the United States. While Ali was known for his brash and playful public persona, which earned him the nickname the "Louisville Lip," people still had to take seriously his sophisticated analyses of contemporary political issues. The combination of his persona and his politics fundamentally transformed the image of the black athlete.

Ali returned to the professional boxing circuit in October 1970. After suffering his first professional defeat to Joe Frazier in March 1971, Ali fought in a series of legendary fights against George Foreman, Ken Norton, and Leon Spinks. He regained the heavyweight crown from Foreman in October 1974, and then from Spinks in September 1978. Ali left the ring for good in 1981 with a professional record of 56 wins and 5 losses. He lives on a farm near Berrien Springs, Michigan. Despite suffering from Parkinson's syndrome, Ali continues to travel and make public appearances around the country.

PUBLICATION
The Greatest: My Own Story (1975)

FURTHER READING
Gorn, Elliott J., ed. *Muhammad Ali, The People's Champ.* Urbana: University of Illinois Press, 1995.
Hauser, Thomas. *Muhammad Ali in Perspective.* San Francisco: Collins, 1996.
Rummel, Jack. *Muhammad Ali.* New York: Chelsea House, 1988.
Sammons, Jeffrey T. *Beyond the Ring: The Role of Boxing in American Society.* Urbana: University of Illinois Press, 1988.

Allen, Richard
ABOLITIONIST, FOUNDER OF THE AFRICAN
METHODIST EPISCOPAL CHURCH

Born: February 14, 1760
Philadelphia, Pennsylvania

Died: March 26, 1831
Philadelphia, Pennsylvania

Allen was born enslaved to a Quaker lawyer and was later sold, along with his family, to a man who lived near Dover, Delaware. At 17 he had a religious conversion experience while listening to a black preacher, Freeborn Garrettson. After gaining his freedom in 1781, Allen wandered across Pennsylvania, New Jersey, and Maryland, preaching and performing manual labor. Within a year of joining a Methodist society, he became the first African American licensed to preach in the Methodist church.

In 1786 Allen joined a predominantly white congregation, St. George's Methodist Episcopal Church in Philadelphia. The following year, he and several other blacks walked out of St. George's during services when white congregants denied them the right to worship on the main floor. Allen quickly set out to establish an independent black congregation, building in part upon a non-sectarian religious organization, the Free African Society, that he and Absalom Jones had founded earlier that year. In 1794 he founded an all-black Methodist congregation in Philadelphia, the Bethel Church.

In 1799, Allen was ordained as a Methodist deacon, becoming the first African American to achieve this status. Yet despite this recognition, the Methodist church forbade Allen from participating in its leadership meetings. In response, Allen and members of the Free African Society established the African Methodist Episcopal (AME) Church. The courts recognized the AME the following year, making it the first legally recognized black church that was independent of white control.

The creation of the AME encouraged the trend in many black communities, north and south, toward establishing independent congregations. It also made Allen one of the first nationally recognized black leaders, a position he used to publicly attack slavery and racism. Like many African Americans, Allen saw these new churches as institutions that could apply religious teachings to the challenges facing blacks, both free and enslaved. The AME and other independent black churches supported antislavery movements and provided refuge for fugitive slaves. Allen, Jones, and others organized against the American Colonization Society, a group that encouraged the deportation of free and enslaved blacks to Africa. And

they supported the Free Produce Society, an organization that distributed goods only if they were produced by free laborers.

In 1830, just months before his death, Allen helped organize a convention of 40 black leaders from throughout the North to discuss the state of American blacks. The meeting—the first black convention in American history— initiated what would develop into the Negro Convention Movement.

FURTHER READING

George, Carol V. R. *Segregated Sabbaths: Richard Allen and the Emergence of Independent Black Churches, 1760–1840*. New York: Oxford University Press, 1973.
Klots, Steve. *Richard Allen*. New York: Chelsea House, 1990.

Anderson, Marian

SINGER, HUMAN RIGHTS ACTIVIST

*Born: February 27, 1897
Philadelphia, Pennsylvania*

*Died: April 8, 1993
Portland, Oregon*

Marian Anderson believed that her voice and the ability to use it in song was a gift from God that she wanted to share with all people. As an internationally acclaimed contralto, she shared her gift with millions singing Negro spirituals and European classical music. She also used her voice to speak out against oppression in the United States. Anderson began singing at six, when she joined her church's junior choir. Once she reached high school she took weekly music classes and joined the high school choir. In 1919 she sang at the meeting of the National Baptist

Convention under the direction of the accomplished gospel composer Lucie Campbell. At 21 she performed a debut recital at Town Hall in New York City. The poor attendance and her mediocre performance caused her to retreat from singing for more than a year.

Most white venues were not ready for a black woman concert singer. Frustrated by this situation, Anderson left for England for further study and performance opportunities. After a fellowship to study in Germany and a Scandinavian concert tour, Anderson returned to Town Hall in 1935, where her three-octave range thrilled the audience. It was in 1939, however, that she reached her largest audience. Howard University sought a venue to present Marian Anderson in Washington, D.C., as part of its concert series. The use of Constitution Hall (the major concert hall in Washington, D.C.), which was run by the Daughters of the American Revolution (DAR), was denied because the DAR prohibited Negroes from performing in the hall. The Marian Anderson Citizens Committee (MACC), chaired by Charles Hamilton Houston, was formed. A flyer put out by the MACC stated, "The DAR would not let her sing in Constitution Hall . . . but under the auspices of the Howard University, Marian Anderson sings free in the open air to the people of Washington, Easter Sunday, April 9, at the Lincoln Memorial." Anderson's opening song, with the Howard University Choir behind her, was "America."

In addition to singing, Anderson used her influence in other arenas. From 1958 to 1959, she served as a United Nations alternate delegate, and she pushed for a special session of the General Assembly to address the independence of Cameroon, a West African nation. Marian Anderson gave her farewell performance in Carnegie Hall in New York in 1965.

PUBLICATION
My Lord, What a Morning: An Autobiography (1956)

FURTHER READING
Patterson, Charles. *Marian Anderson.* New York: Watts, 1988.
Tedards, Anne. *Marian Anderson.* New York: Chelsea House, 1988.

Angelou, Maya
WRITER, ACTRESS

Born: April 4, 1928
St. Louis, Missouri

Born Marguerite Johnson in 1928, Maya Angelou grew up with her paternal grandmother in Stamps, Arkansas, and later, as a teenager, lived with her mother in San Francisco. She attended George Washington High School and studied drama and dance at the California Labor School. While raising her son (born when Angelou was 16), she worked a variety of jobs—including streetcar conductor, cook, and nightclub waitress—before becoming a professional dancer.

In 1954 she toured Europe and Africa with a production of *Porgy and Bess,* and in 1961 appeared in Jean Genet's *The Blacks.* She also helped raise money for the civil rights movement and served as the northern coordinator for the Southern Christian Leadership Conference between 1959 and 1960. After living in Ghana with her son during the early

1960s, Angelou returned to the United States and began publishing the poetry and stories for which she is best known.

In 1970, her autobiographical account of her childhood in Arkansas, *I Know Why the Caged Bird Sings,* quickly became a best-seller. In this and much of her writing, she explores her experience of growing up a black woman in the United States. She has since published four more volumes of autobiography as well as several collections of poetry (including *Just Give Me a Cool Drink of Water 'fore I Diiie*, for which she received a Pulitzer Prize nomination). At President Bill Clinton's request, she composed and read the poem "On the Pulse of a New Morning" at his January 1993 inauguration.

SELECTED PUBLICATIONS
I Know Why the Caged Bird Sings (1970)
Just Give Me a Cool Drink of Water 'fore I Diiie (1971)
The Heart of a Woman (1982)
I Shall Not be Moved (1990)
Wouldn't Take Nothing for My Journey Now (1993)

FURTHER READING
Lisandrelli, Elaine. *Maya Angelou: More Than a Poet.* Springfield, N.J.: Enslow, 1996.

◇ ◇ ◇
Armstrong, Louis ("Satchmo," "Pops")
TRUMPETER, SINGER, BAND LEADER

Born: August 4, 1900
New Orleans, Louisiana

Died: July 6, 1971
New York, New York

Raised by his maternal grandmother and later by his mother, Louis Armstrong grew up in an impoverished New Orleans neighborhood. He grew up surrounded by African-American music; artists such as Buddy Bolden and Bunk Johnson performed blues and early jazz in local dance halls and saloons. Armstrong sang in the neighborhood churches and later performed in the streets with a vocal quartet. At the age of 12, he was arrested for delinquency (the specific reasons are unclear) and sent to the Colored Waifs' Home. At the orphanage Armstrong received some formal music training and was introduced to several instruments, including the cornet.

Released from the Home at the age of 14, Armstrong worked odd jobs and borrowed a cornet to play local clubs. He soon befriended Joe "King" Oliver, one of the most influential early jazz musicians, who gave the young Armstrong his first cornet and instructed him on it. Armstrong soon began to play professionally in New Orleans. He played on riverboats with Fate Marable's prominent band and replaced Oliver as cornet player in Kid Ory's band when Oliver moved to Chicago in 1919. Three years later, Armstrong accepted Oliver's invitation to play second cornet in his influential Creole Jazz Band in Chicago.

Armstrong's musicianship—his inventive placement of accents, his powerful sense of "swing"—soon had a tremendous impact on artists who heard him live or on recordings. In 1924 he moved to New York City to join Fletcher Henderson's big band, and he recorded with artists such as Bessie Smith, Ma Rainey, and Alberta Hunter. The next year, he returned to Chicago, where he formed the Hot Five (later the Hot Seven)—which included his wife Lil Hardin on piano—and recorded with other groups as well.

In recordings made over the next several years, Armstrong quickly established an international reputation. The sensitivity of his playing, and his rhythmic and harmonic innovations from this period have had a tremendous influence on the history of jazz composition and performance. During the 1920s, he experimented with a range of styles and formats, including traditional New Orleans ensemble play, small group sessions, and finally a big band, with which he worked from 1929 to 1947. Armstrong made some of the first recordings of "scat" singing. And his emotional and unorthodox interpretations of popular songs—whether sung or played on cornet—have had an enduring impact on jazz vocalists to this day.

In the 1940s, many young jazz musicians came to see Armstrong's music and his manner as old-fashioned—even degrading to African Americans. Still, Armstrong's recordings, his performances, and his appearances in nearly 50 films introduced millions of people to jazz for decades to come. From 1947 until his death in 1971, he played, recorded and toured the world with a sextet, the All Stars. The group's international travels in the 1960s earned Armstrong the nickname "Ambassador Satch."

PUBLICATIONS
Swing that Music (1937)
Satchmo: My Life in New Orleans (1954)
Louis Armstrong: A Self-Portrait (1971)

FURTHER READING
Jones, Max, and John Chilton. *Louis: The Louis Armstrong Story, 1900–1971.* Boston: Little, Brown, 1971.
Tanenhaus, Sam. *Louis Armstrong.* New York: Chelsea House, 1989.

Baker, Ella
ACTIVIST, EDUCATOR, JOURNALIST

Born: December 13, 1903
Norfolk, Virginia

Died: December 13, 1986
New York, New York

The granddaughter of former slaves, Ella Baker attended public schools in Littleton, North Carolina, and later graduated as valedictorian of her 1927 class from Shaw University in Raleigh, North Carolina. She was an outstanding debater in school and a vocal critic of racist school policies.

After college, Baker moved to Harlem, where she wrote for newspapers and supported local reform efforts. In 1931, she was elected the first national director of the newly created Young Negro Cooperative League and helped to establish buying clubs and cooperative groceries for blacks in Philadelphia and Chicago. She met a number of other radical activists in the 1930s through her work at the Federal Workers' Education Project.

In the early 1940s, Baker worked as a field organizer for the National Association for the Advancement of Colored People, and she served as its "director of branches" from 1943 until 1946. Baker helped establish a wide-ranging network of community groups and contacts throughout the South that would help form the foundation for the postwar civil rights movement. She left her paid position in the NAACP in protest, convinced that the organization was too bureaucratic and hierarchical, and frustrated that its leadership was unwilling to experiment with more confrontational tactics.

In the late 1950s, Baker moved to the South, where she organized mass meetings for the Southern Christian Leadership Conference (SCLC). She set up SCLC's Atlanta office and coordinated its voting rights campaign, the Crusade for Citizenship. Baker eventually grew impatient with the conservatism of SCLC, fearing that the organization's established leadership would undermine the student movement by taming its radicalism. She left the organization to work at a local YMCA and in 1960 convinced Shaw University to host a conference for student activists committed to challenging segregation with nonviolent direct action. At this conference, the Student Nonviolent Coordinating Committee (SNCC) was born. With other SNCC members, Baker helped found the Mississippi Freedom Democratic Party, which registered voters and challenged the state's all-white party primaries.

Baker remained involved in politics throughout her life, supporting and advising numerous coalitions, activists, and public officials. She influenced countless women and men who became leaders in civil rights struggles and in American electoral politics. Through her commitment to a politics that was truly democratic and responsive to community needs, she helped to sustain radical African-American activism in the 20th century.

FURTHER READING

Dallard, Shyrlee. *Ella Baker: A Leader Behind the Scenes*. Englewood Cliffs, N.J.: Silver Burdett, 1990.
Payne, Charles. "Ella Baker and Models of Social Change," *SIGNS*, Summer 1989.

Baldwin, James
WRITER

Born: August 2, 1924
New York, New York

Died: November 30, 1987
St. Paul de Vence, France

Baldwin's novels, essays, plays, short stories, and poetry constitute one of the most important contributions to 20th-century American letters. Drawing upon a variety of literary traditions and everyday experiences—ranging from church sermons, the blues, and conversations overheard on the streets of Harlem to the King James Bible and Dostoyevsky—Baldwin wrote about the lives of black Americans and the legacy of racism and sexism in American society.

The oldest of nine children, Baldwin was raised in Harlem by his mother, Emma Berdis Jones, and her husband, David Baldwin, who was a laborer and preacher. From an early age he wrote stories, short novels, poems, and plays, several of which appeared in school publications. He preached in the Pentecostal church from ages 14 to 17. Baldwin graduated from DeWitt Clinton High School in the Bronx in 1941.

Unable to afford college, Baldwin worked as a railroad hand and at other jobs to support his family. He eventually moved to Greenwich Village in New York City. With financial help from artists such as Richard Wright, Baldwin wrote book reviews and essays that were published in prominent journals. In 1948 he moved to Paris, where he wrote two very influential essays, "Everybody's Protest Novel" (1949) and "Many Thousands Gone" (1951), both of which were later included in the collection *Notes of a Native Son* (1955). In 1953 he published one of his most acclaimed novels, *Go Tell It on the Mountain*.

In the 1950s and 1960s Baldwin wrote, traveled extensively, and returned to the United States to participate in civil rights protests. In 1963 he published an influential and controversial essay, *The Fire Next Time*, which explores the legacy of white racism in the United States. His writings on male sexuality, and his openness about his own bisexuality, made Baldwin an important inspiration to the growing gay rights movement. As a result of his political activity and the controversial nature of his writings, the Federal Bureau of Investigation monitored Baldwin's activities throughout the 1960s and early 1970s.

His other work from this period includes a screenplay depicting the life of Malcolm X (1972) and a history of blacks in film (*The Devil Finds Work*, 1976). Beginning in 1982, he taught writing and African-American history at the University of Massachusetts, Amherst.

Dividing his time between France and the United States, he continued to teach, lecture, and publish until succumbing to cancer in 1987.

SELECTED PUBLICATIONS
Go Tell It on the Mountain (1953)
Notes of a Native Son (1955)
Another Country (1962)
The Fire Next Time (1963)
The Price of the Ticket (1985)

FURTHER READING
Campbell, James. *Talking at the Gates: A Life of James Baldwin*. Boston: Faber & Faber, 1991.
Leeming, David. *James Baldwin: A Biography*. New York: Knopf, 1994.
Rosset, Lisa. *James Baldwin*. New York: Chelsea House, 1989.

Baraka, Amiri (LeRoi Jones)
WRITER, ACTIVIST

Born: October 7, 1934
Newark, New Jersey

"The only constant in life is in change." This sentence effectively captures the philosophy of Amiri Baraka. Baraka, born Everett Leroy Jones, has had a prolific career as a poet, essayist, lecturer, and editor. Since the 1950s, Baraka has used his writing to critique American politics and culture.

Jones grew up in a racially mixed neighborhood and excelled at his predominantly white high school. He studied at Rutgers, then Howard University, gathering inspiration at Howard from the poet and literary critic Sterling Brown. Jones dropped out of Howard in 1953 and joined the air force.

After his discharge, Jones moved to Greenwich Village in New York to become a writer. His first published essay was a defense of the Beat writers—mostly white male writers who decried the emphasis in American society on material wealth and conservatism. He met Hettie Cohen, a white Jewish woman, whom he married in 1958. The late 1950s and early 1960s proved to be a turning point in Jones's life. In 1959 he traveled to Cuba with a delegation of black scholars and artists and praised the Cuban Revolution. Upon his return, he began to write more directly about black and political themes. In 1965 he changed his name to Amiri Baraka, left his wife and two daughters, and moved to Harlem.

In Harlem, Baraka cofounded the Black Arts Repertory Theater School, a theater and cultural center. After the theater lost its federal funding, Baraka moved back to Newark and founded Spirit House, a cultural center that emphasized cultural nationalism—adoption of traditional African dress, language, and values. The Newark to which Baraka relocated had the largest number of condemned houses and the highest crime rate in the nation and an unemployment rate that was twice as high as the national rate. A little more than half the population was black, approximately 12 percent were Puerto Rican, and city politics was dominated by Italian Americans. All of these ingredients helped to spawn an uprising in 1967. Jones was picked up by the police for resisting arrest and for unlawful possession of firearms. After a week in prison he was released on appeal. This experience propelled him to more direct political action.

In 1968 Baraka organized the Committee for a New Ark and called a convention to nominate black candidates for the city council. Two years later a black man, Kenneth Gibson, was elected mayor of Newark. Baraka, however, became disillusioned with conventional politics after Gibson began to treat Puerto Ricans unfairly and because he felt other black leaders failed to push the National Black Agenda. Baraka later rejected black nationalism and adopted socialism. He continues to write and lecture.

SELECTED PUBLICATIONS
Preface to a Twenty Volume Suicide Note (1961)
Blues People: Negro Music in White America (1963)
The System of Dante's Hell (1964)
The Autobiography of LeRoi Jones/Amiri Baraka (1984)
Transbluecency (1995)

FURTHER READING
Baraka, Imamu Amiri. *The LeRoi Jones/Amiri Baraka Reader*. Edited by William J. Harris in collaboration with Amiri Baraka. New York: Thunder's Mouth, 1991.
Bernotas, Bob. *Amiri Baraka.* New York: Chelsea House, 1991.
Brown, Lloyd W. *Amiri Baraka.* Boston: Twayne, 1980.

Bethune, Mary McLeod

EDUCATOR, CIVIL RIGHTS LEADER, FEDERAL OFFICIAL

Born: July 10, 1875
Mayesville, South Carolina

Died: May 18, 1955
Daytona Beach, Florida

Mary McLeod Bethune was born just a decade after emancipation; her parents and her 16 older sisters and brothers had been born into slavery. She and her siblings grew up working with their parents on their family's small farm. At a time when it was virtually impossible for black children in the South to get an education, Bethune learned to read when a black missionary sent by the northern Presbyterian church opened a school nearby. Scholarships enabled her to attend the Scotia Seminary in Concord, North Carolina, and then the Moody Bible School in Chicago, where she trained to do missionary work in Africa. When her applications to do missionary work were rejected, Bethune accepted a teaching position at Haines Institute in Augusta, Georgia, in 1896.

In 1904, Bethune moved to Daytona Beach, Florida, and lived with friends while raising money to transform a small cottage that she had purchased into an independent school. By

October of that year, she enrolled five children in the new Daytona Educational and Industrial Institute. The school was destitute for many years, but Bethune eventually raised enough money and support to purchase additional properties and to construct modern facilities. The Institute emphasized vocational training at first, and later developed a teacher-training program. In 1922, Cookman College, a men's school in Jacksonville, merged with the Daytona Institute, creating the coeducational Bethune Cookman College.

Bethune's other commitments were numerous. Principal among them was her leadership within the black women's club movement. In 1924, after working for years with state and regional organizations, she was elected president of the National Association of Colored Women (NACW). Under Bethune's leadership, the NACW supported the fight for federal anti-lynching legislation, designed programs to assist rural and urban working women, and addressed the problems facing women of color in other nations. In 1935 Bethune helped found the National Council of Negro Women (NCNW), and she served as its president until 1949. At the NCNW, Bethune stressed the necessity of creating policy-making and management positions for black women in the federal government.

In 1936 President Franklin D. Roosevelt appointed Bethune administrator of the Negro division of the National Youth Administration, which she directed for seven years. In January 1937 Bethune brought together government officials and the leaders of black organizations for a National Conference on the Problems of the Negro and Negro Youth. Bethune later served as special assistant to the Secretary of War during World War II and as an adviser to the U.S. commission that participated in drafting the United Nations Charter.

FURTHER READING
Halasa, Malu. *Mary McLeod Bethune*. New York: Chelsea House, 1989.

Bradley, Thomas
POLITICIAN, ACTIVIST, POLICE OFFICER

Born: December 29, 1917
Calvert, Texas

Tom Bradley was the son of Lee Bradley and Crenner Hawkins, who worked as sharecroppers in Calvert, Texas. Poverty forced the family to move several times during Tom's childhood, first to Dallas, Texas, then to Somerton, Arizona, and finally to Los Angeles in 1924. Their living conditions were so dire that five of his siblings died of poor health as children. Tom began selling newspapers at age 10 to help support the family.

Following an outstanding academic and athletic career at Los Angeles's Polytechnic High School, Bradley won a scholarship to UCLA. In 1941 he entered the Police Academy, and served on the Los Angeles Police Department (LAPD) for the next 20 years, reaching the rank of lieutenant. During his time with the LAPD, Bradley earned a reputation in the community as an outspoken defender of the rights of blacks, Mexican Americans, and other minority populations. He supported local Democratic campaigns, helped organize against racial segregation within the LAPD, and worked with dozens of clubs and organizations. He also attended law school at night and passed the California bar in 1956. Five years later he left the LAPD to practice law.

Soon thereafter he was elected to the city council, representing Los Angeles's predominantly white 10th District from 1963 to 1973. After the 1965 Watts riots, Bradley criticized the police for their brutal treatment of minorities, a stance that led to a public battle with the LAPD and the city's white mayor, Sam Yorty.

Nevertheless, Bradley remained popular among Los Angeles's white voters, in part because of his record of public service and also because whites considered him a moderate. In 1969, Bradley beat Yorty in the primary election for mayor. Yorty won the runoff election by depicting Bradley as "un-American" and linking him to "militant" black leaders. Four years later Bradley defeated Yorty, becoming Los Angeles's first black mayor and the first African-American mayor of a city with a predominantly white population. He was reelected four times, serving until 1993.

Bradley was credited with numerous successes during his tenure—including the city's hosting of the 1984 Olympic Games—but was also criticized for pursuing policies that hurt the city's working classes, and for promoting urban redevelopment schemes that undermined inner city neighborhoods. Bradley also came under heavy criticism from both black and white voters following the March 1991 beating of Rodney King by LAPD officers and the 1992 riot that followed the officers' acquittal.

Bradley served on the board of directors of the Los Angeles Branch of the Urban League and as a trustee of the First AME Church. He ran unsuccessfully for governor of California in 1982 and 1986.

FURTHER READING
Payne, Gregory J., and Scott Ratsan. *Tom Bradley: The Impossible Dream*. Santa Monica, Calif.: Roundtable, 1986.

Briggs, Cyril

BLACK NATIONALIST, JOURNALIST

Born: 1888
Nevis Island, British West Indies

Died: October 18, 1966
Los Angeles, California

Cyril Briggs, a Communist party member and leader of the African Blood Brotherhood for African Liberation and Redemption, worked most of his life as a journalist. His training began as a student, when he worked for two of his hometown newspapers. After he migrated to the United States in 1905, he worked for the *Amsterdam News*, one of the major black newspapers in the country. In his editorials, Briggs became increasingly critical of how the United States treated African-American soldiers during World War I. Deemed inflammatory by the U.S. Post Office, Briggs's articles were often censored.

Briggs decided to stop working at the *Amsterdam News* and began working full-time on the *Crusader*, a newspaper he started in 1918. Briggs was now free to condemn the United States for its antidemocratic actions as well as to advance his own political opinions.

Briggs announced the African Blood Brotherhood (ABB) to *Crusader* readers in

1919. It was founded in reaction to the numerous race riots that took place throughout the country that summer. The ABB is believed to be the first organization to advocate armed self-defense. Because of the deaths and injuries that resulted from riots and lynchings, as well as the daily harassment felt by civilians and soldiers, Briggs believed that violence should be met with violence. The initial focus of the ABB was self-government for the Negro and a theme of Africa for the Africans (similar to Marcus Garvey's UNIA-ACL). The organization evolved from a complete emphasis on Africa and race to advocate the importance of class and a workers' revolution. The ABB was aligned with the Communist party (CPUSA) and served as a vehicle to recruit other African Americans into the CPUSA.

After the ABB was dissolved in the mid-1920s, Briggs remained active as a Communist party member. In 1938 he was forced to leave the CPUSA because of disagreements with other party members. Six years later he moved to Los Angeles, joined the local CPUSA, and worked as an editor for the *Los Angeles Herald-Dispatch*.

FURTHER READING
Hill, Robert A., ed. *The Crusader*. 3 volumes. New York: Garland, 1987.

Brown, James

SINGER, SONGWRITER

Born: May 3, 1933
Barnwell, South Carolina

James Brown began playing drums, piano, harmonica, and organ at a young age. He left school in the seventh grade and per-

formed with various gospel groups before starting his first musical group, the Cremona Trio. This band played rhythm and blues, a popular form of music developed after World War II that emphasized up-tempo, fast-paced rhythms.

Brown and his family struggled financially during most of his young life. He held a number of odd jobs, often resorting to petty theft. In 1949 he was caught and imprisoned at the Georgia Juvenile Technical Institute. After he was released, he joined the Gospel Starlighters, which later switched to rhythm and blues and became the Flames. The transition from gospel to secular music, which became common for many musicians in the 1950s and 1960s who wanted to appeal to a larger audience, led to the creation of a new form of r&b called soul music. Artists such as Ray Charles, Sam Cooke, and Aretha Franklin used the inflection and emotion of gospel for such secular topics as romantic love and black power.

By 1965 Brown was the number one rhythm and blues artist in the country. He achieved that status by touring constantly and giving himself completely to his audiences, which led to the titles "the hardest working man in show business" and "the Godfather of soul." With songs such as "Please, Please, Please," "Papa's Got a Brand New Bag," and "Say It Loud, I'm Black and I'm Proud," Brown put into words, music, and dance what millions of African Americans were feeling and protesting about their experiences in the United States. Brown became an important icon for citizens involved in the black power and civil rights movements. His decision to grow an Afro and his accumulation of wealth were visible signs of the immense possibilities for the future.

Brown continues to tour. In the 1980s, his work was often sampled by hip hop musicians who used his lyrics and music in their own songs.

FURTHER READING

Brown, James, with Bruce Tucker. *James Brown: The Godfather of Soul*. New York: Macmillan, 1986.
Rose, Cynthia. *Living in America: The Soul Saga of James Brown*. London: Serpent's Tail, 1990.

Bunche, Ralph J.

SCHOLAR, ACTIVIST, GOVERNMENT OFFICIAL

Born: August 7, 1904
Detroit, Michigan

Died: December 9, 1971
New York, New York

Bunche was born in 1904 to Fred and Olive Johnson Bunch (Ralph added the "e" to his name as a young adult). He grew up in poverty—first in Detroit, then in Cleveland and Toledo, Ohio, and Albuquerque, New Mexico. His parents died when he was 12, forcing Ralph, his grandmother, sister, and two aunts to move to Los Angeles. Bunche graduated first in his class from Jefferson High School, with awards in debate, composition, and civics and with letters in basketball, football, and baseball. He attended the University of California at Los Angeles on an athletic scholarship and graduated as valedictorian in 1922 with numerous academic honors and a degree in international relations.

After a local black women's organization raised $1,000 to pay for his moving expenses, Bunche accepted a scholarship to study political science and philosophy at Harvard University. While working on his degree there, he taught courses at Howard University in Washington, D.C., and traveled to several West African countries to study their political development. By 1934, Bunche had earned his Ph.D. and had helped establish the first department of political science at Howard.

Bunche engaged in civil rights struggles throughout his life. For example, he organized a protest against segregation in Washington, D.C.'s National Theater in 1931. In 1936, he helped found the National Negro Congress and became codirector of the Swarthmore College Institute of Race Relations, where he published *A World View of Race* in 1937. Between 1938 and 1940 he collaborated with Swedish sociologist Gunnar Myrdal on the research that would produce Myrdal's *American Dilemma* (1944), one of the most important modern works on race relations in the United States. Years later, in 1964, Bunche joined thousands of civil rights protestors in the march from Selma to Montgomery.

With the onset of World War II, Bunche began a distinguished career in government service. He worked for the Office for Strategic Services, then as an Africa specialist for the State Department. After the war he played a key role in the meetings that led to the establishment of the United Nations and to the drafting of the UN Charter. Bunche was instrumental in defining the UN's peacekeeping mission, and later helped facilitate UN peacekeeping efforts in the Middle East, Zaire, and Cyprus. In 1950, Bunche received the Nobel Peace Prize for his efforts toward finding a resolution to the first Israeli-Arab war. In 1967 he became undersecretary general of the United Nations.

SELECTED PUBLICATION
A World View of Race (1937)

FURTHER READING
Urquhart, Brian. *Ralph Bunche: An American Life*. New York: Norton, 1993.

Carmichael, Stokely (Kwame Touré)

ACTIVIST, AUTHOR

Born: June 29, 1941
Port of Spain, Trinidad

When he was eight years old, Stokely Carmichael immigrated with his family from Trinidad to New York City. After graduating from the Bronx High School of Science in 1960, he moved to Washington, D.C., to attend Howard University, where he studied philosophy and explored his interest in black nationalism. He graduated with honors in 1964.

During his first year at Howard, Carmichael participated in a wide range of civil rights activities, including the Freedom Rides and a protest against the House Committee on Un-American Activities. He soon joined the Student Nonviolent Coordinating Committee (SNCC) and helped organize the Mississippi Freedom Democratic Party. By the mid-1960s, Carmichael grew disillusioned with the mainstream civil rights movement. He helped lead

SNCC in a formal break with the nonviolent movement and helped to popularize the ideas and strategies of what came to be known as Black Power.

In their 1967 book *Black Power: The Politics of Liberation in America*, Carmichael and co-author Charles Hamilton offered a radical analysis of political institutions and political power in the United States. The only means by which blacks could liberate themselves from their "colonial" status, they argued, was by forging all-black political coalitions, community institutions, and economic networks. The authors rejected the strategies of mainstream black leaders and the goal of assimilation "into middle class America," insisting that blacks be prepared to meet white racist violence with violence of their own.

Established civil rights leaders dismissed Carmichael's work as inflammatory and quickly distanced themselves from the Black Power movement as a whole. Carmichael bred further controversy when he publicly denounced U.S. involvement in Vietnam and attacked the Zionist movement during the 1967 Arab-Israeli war.

Carmichael encouraged blacks to form alliances with subjugated peoples worldwide. He helped organize migrant farm laborers during the late 1960s and supported the struggle of Native Americans to reclaim their ancestral lands. As a representative of SNCC, he traveled to Puerto Rico, North Vietnam, the Middle East, Africa, Cuba, and several European nations.

In February 1968, Carmichael was invited by Huey Newton, Bobby Seale, and Eldridge Cleaver to serve as prime minister of the Black Panther party. Later that year, SNCC fired Carmichael for ignoring decisions made by its executive body. With his wife, singer Miriam Makeba, Carmichael moved to Guinea, where he studied with prominent Pan-Africanists. Upon his return to the United States in 1972, he publicized the formation of an All African People's Revolutionary Party. Divorced from Makeba in 1979, Carmichael (now Kwame Touré) has lived mostly in Guinea, where he remarried. Because he suffers from prostate cancer, he now spends much of his time in hospitals in Cuba and the United States.

SELECTED PUBLICATION
Black Power: The Politics of Liberation in America (1967, with Charles V. Hamilton)

FURTHER READING
Carson, Clayborne. *In Struggle: SNCC and the Black Awakening of the 1960s.* Cambridge: Harvard University Press, 1981.
Johnson, Jacqueline. *Stokely Carmichael: The Story of Black Power.* Englewood Cliffs, N.J.: Silver Burdett, 1990.

Carver, George Washington

SCIENTIST, EDUCATOR

*Born: About 1864
Diamond, Missouri*

*Died: January 5, 1943
Tuskegee, Alabama*

George Washington Carver, born enslaved, became internationally known for his scientific ingenuity, including the development of over 300 industrial uses for the peanut and sweet potato. Carver was fascinated by the wonders of nature and chose to live a simple, nonmaterialistic life, despite his fame and contributions to developing technologies.

Like many other enslaved persons, Carver did not know the date of his birth or his family name. His father died when he was young and he was separated from his mother after they were both kidnapped from the plantation they were living on. He was raised by German-American farmers Moses and Susan Carver, his mother's former slaveowners.

Carver's formal education took place in numerous schools and cities. He went to Kansas for high school but did not stay there long. He worked to raise money for school while receiving an erratic education. After one year at Simpson College in Indianola, Iowa, as an art student, he transferred to Iowa Agricultural College (now Iowa State) in Ames, Iowa. After receiving bachelor's and master's degrees, he began teaching agricultural chemistry at the college. At Iowa Agricultural, his research specialties included mycology (the study of fungi) and plant cross-fertilization.

Booker T. Washington, president of Tuskegee Normal and Industrial Institute (now Tuskegee University), invited Carver to join the faculty as head of the agriculture department. In addition to his research and teaching at Tuskegee, Carver offered his expertise to area farmers and sharecroppers by writing and distributing educational agriculture bulletins and meeting with them to determine the most beneficial and lucrative crops.

Carver, while a serious researcher, was no businessman. He refused to patent any of his research findings. He felt it inappropriate that he profit from what was given to him (and the world) by God.

FURTHER READING
Adair, Gene. *George Washington Carver.* New York: Chelsea House, 1989.
Kremer, Gary R., ed. *George Washington Carver in His Own Words.* Columbia: University of Missouri Press, 1987.
McMurry, Linda O. *George Washington Carver: Scientist and Symbol.* New York: Oxford University Press, 1981.

Chisholm, Shirley

POLITICIAN, EDUCATOR

Born: November 30, 1924
Brooklyn, New York

Shirley Chisholm was born Shirley St. Hill in 1924. Her mother, Ruby Seale, was a seamstress and a native of Barbados. Her father, Charles St. Hill, was a baker's helper and factory hand born in British Guiana and raised in Cuba and Barbados. Shirley spent several years on the family farm in Barbados with her sisters, cousins, mother and grandmother before returning to New York at age 10.

After completing high school, Shirley attended Brooklyn College and became increasingly involved in local political activities. She graduated cum laude in 1946, then worked as a teacher's aide in Harlem and earned a master's degree in education from Teachers College at Columbia University. She also became an influential member of the local Democratic party organization, where she focused on the rights of blacks and women within the party. In 1949, she married Conrad Chisholm.

In 1960 Shirley Chisholm helped form the Unity Democratic Club in New York, which challenged the mainstream Democratic organization by running black candidates in local elections. Four years later, she was elected to the New York State Assembly. As an assemblywoman, Chisholm fought for increased public school spending and sponsored legislation protecting the rights of poor and disabled students, working mothers, domestic workers, and school teachers. In 1968 she was elected to the U.S. House of Representatives, becoming the first African-American woman to hold a seat in Congress. In January 1971, Chisholm announced her candidacy for the Democratic Presidential nomination—the first African American to do so.

As a congresswoman Chisholm focused on issues of economic justice, education, and the rights of women and minorities. In the early 1970s she was an outspoken opponent of U.S. involvement in Vietnam. During her final term in Congress, she was a vocal critic of the Reagan administration's spending cuts for social service programs.

Chisholm retired from the House of Representatives in 1982. Since then she has taught political science and women's studies at Mount Holyoke College and Spelman College and lectured around the country. Chisholm was a founding member of the National Political Congress of Black Women.

PUBLICATIONS
Unbought and Unbossed (1970)
The Good Fight (1973)

FURTHER READING
Scheader, Catherine. *Shirley Chisholm: Teacher and Congresswoman.* Hillside, N.J.: Enslow, 1990.

Clinton, George

MUSICIAN

Born: July 22, 1941
Kannapolis, North Carolina

The man whose name would become synonymous with the music known as "funk" grew up in Plainsfield, New Jersey. When he was 14, George Clinton formed a doo-wop group called The Parliaments and supported himself by working full time, including a job as a hairdresser. The Parliaments made a few recordings in the late 1950s, none of which sold very well. In the mid-1960s, Clinton also worked for Motown Records as a staff songwriter.

In 1966 The Parliaments recorded "(I Wanna) Testify," a single that was both a commercial success (it made the Top 20 in 1967) and a musical departure for the band. Clinton soon added horns and electric instruments to The Parliaments and in 1969 formed another group, Funkadelic (the membership of the two bands was often overlapping). During the 1970s, the bands often recorded together under the name Parliament Funkadelic (commonly known as "P-Funk").

During the 1970s, Clinton's bands—which included former James Brown sidemen Maceo Parker and William "Bootsy" Collins—became the premier funk acts. Inspired by the funk and soul of James Brown's music, P-Funk took the music in new directions. With imaginative songwriting, virtuoso musicianship, and outrageous stage performances, the bands fused funk beats and rhythm and blues harmonies with psychedelic rock. The bands borrowed from numerous musical traditions, ranging from soul to heavy metal to jazz. Some of the artists that influenced P-Funk's music and style include The Temptations, Iggy Pop, Sly Stone, David Bowie and Jimi Hendrix. The result is not necessarily a form of music, as Clinton explains, but rather a "kind of an attitude." Funk, according to Clinton, is "anything it need to be to save your life."

Clinton and P-Funk reached the height of their popularity in the mid-1970s with albums such as *Mothership Connection* (1975), *Standing on the Verge of Getting It On* (1974), and *One Nation Under a Groove* (1978). Clinton's recordings continue to have an enormous influence on hip hop and rock. His recent recordings have featured artists including Ice Cube, Yo Yo, Dr. Dre, and jazz pianist Herbie Hancock.

FURTHER READING
Vincent, Rickey. *Funk: The Music, the People, and the Rhythm of the One.* New York: St. Martin's, 1996.

Cosby, Bill (William H. Cosby, Jr.)
COMEDIAN, ACTOR, PRODUCER, AUTHOR
Born: July 12, 1937
Germantown, Pennsylvania

While studying physical education at Temple University in Philadelphia in 1963, Bill Cosby began working at a coffeehouse, where he bartended and told jokes. As he became more popular as a performer, he got gigs in New York and eventually left college to pursue a career as a comedian.

Two years after his debut in Philadelphia, he gained a starring role in the television series *I Spy*, about two secret agents. Cosby's role, originally intended for a white actor, was significant because it was one of the earliest representations of a black actor in a dramatic role. Cosby followed *I Spy* with the *Bill Cosby Show* (1969–1971), *Fat Albert and the Cosby Kids* (1972–1979), the *Cosby Show*

(1984–1992), and several other television programs.

Of all these programs, the *Cosby Show* has had the most impact. On the show, Cosby, a pediatrician, lives comfortably in a New York brownstone with his wife, who is a lawyer, and their four children. Though the show was immensely popular, there were mixed reactions to it. Some people applauded the portrayal of a "positive" black family on television; others lambasted the show for not presenting a more "realistic" portrayal of black family life. Despite the differing views, NBC benefited greatly from the success of the show.

In addition to his success on television, Cosby collaborated with actor Sidney Poitier on two films, *Uptown Saturday Night* (1974) and *Let's Do It Again* (1975). In the 1980s he wrote four books, including the popular bestseller *Fatherhood*. Cosby also returned to school and completed his Ph.D. in education at the University of Massachusetts, Amherst.

In 1993 Cosby was listed in *Forbes* magazine as one of the 400 richest people in the world. He has contributed generously to Spelman College, Fisk University, Howard University, and other historically black colleges and universities.

PUBLICATIONS
Fatherhood (1986)
Love and Marriage (1989)
Childhood (1991)

FURTHER READING
Haskins, James. *Bill Cosby: America's Most Famous Father.* New York: Walker, 1988.
Herbert, Solomon J., and George H. Hill. *Bill Cosby.* New York: Chelsea House, 1992.

Cullen, Countee
POET, NOVELIST, PLAYWRIGHT

Born: March 30, 1903
place of birth unknown

Died: January 9, 1946
New York, New York

Very little is known about the childhood of Countee Cullen, one of the most celebrated writers of the 1920s. He was born and spent his early years either in Baltimore, Louisville, or New York City. Then, after his grandmother raised him in New York, he was adopted by the Reverend Frederick A. and Carolyn Belle Mitchell Cullen in 1918. The Rev. Cullen, who led Harlem's Salem Methodist Episcopal Church, was a prominent activist for African-American causes and served as the president of the Harlem chapter of the NAACP.

Countee Cullen enrolled in 1918 at DeWitt Clinton High School, where he edited the school paper and worked on the literary magazine, *Magpie.* During high school Cullen published his first poems and won his first literary contest, a citywide poetry competition. He entered New York University in 1922, graduating Phi Beta Kappa in 1925.

Cullen's early writings showed great promise, earning him several awards and bringing him considerable recognition by the time he attended college. In 1924, *American Mercury* magazine published Cullen's poem "Shroud of Color," confirming his status as an up-and-coming artist. While at New York University he completed most of the work that would comprise his first three published volumes of poetry, the collections *Color* (1925),

Copper Girl (1927), and *The Ballad of the Brown Girl* (1927). By the time he completed a master's degree in English and French literature at Harvard University in 1927, Cullen was the most celebrated black poet in America, a young star of the literary movement often called the Harlem Renaissance. He received many prizes during the 1920s, including an award from *Opportunity* magazine, an Urban League publication that helped promote the new literary movement.

Cullen wrote lyrical poetry, influenced heavily by English romantic verse of the 19th and early 20th centuries. Though his writing about race won him the praise of prominent critics such as Jessie Fauset, Cullen seemed at times uncomfortable that his work was being praised for its political or intellectual content instead of for its emotional power. Some contemporaries criticized Cullen and other writers such as Claude McKay for presenting an idealized, even exotic image of blacks' African past, an image that they feared might be misused by white audiences.

In the 1930s, Cullen devoted most of his time to teaching French to black students at Frederick Douglass Junior High School in New York. He continued to write and publish poetry, including a book of children's verse, and translated writings from French and Greek.

SELECTED PUBLICATIONS
Color (1925)
The Ballad of the Brown Girl (1927)
Copper Girl (1927)
The Lost Zoo (1940)
On These I Stand (1947)

FURTHER READING
Shucard, Alan R. *Countee Cullen.* Boston: Twayne, 1984.

Davis, Angela
ACTIVIST, AUTHOR, EDUCATOR

Born: January 26, 1944
Birmingham, Alabama

Angela Davis grew up in a segregated Birmingham neighborhood famous as a target of white racist violence. From an early age, she was surrounded by family and friends who encouraged her to become involved politically. Her parents were teachers, members of the NAACP, and active supporters of civil rights struggles. At age 15, Angela moved to New York City to attend a progressive private high school, and she lived with a white family dedicated to the civil rights movement. While in New York, Davis joined Advance, a Marxist-Leninist group.

Davis attended Brandeis University in Massachusetts and spent a year studying in Paris, where she befriended a number of Algerian students who were organizing against the French occupation of their homeland. Davis later studied philosophy in Frankfurt, Germany, and participated in a socialist student group. She then earned a master's degree in philosophy at the University of California at San Diego. Davis worked with the Student Nonviolent Coordinating Committee (SNCC) and the Black Panthers in California and became a member of the Communist party in 1968.

The following year Davis was hired by UCLA to teach philosophy, until Governor Ronald Reagan and the University of California Board of Regents fired her, citing a law that forbade the state's employment of members of the Communist party. When the California courts ruled that the law was unconstitutional, the Board of Regents reinstated Davis. However, she was fired again, partly in response to her work with the Black Panthers in defense of black prison inmates.

Soon thereafter, Davis was accused of involvement in a violent outbreak at the Marin County Courthouse. A warrant was issued for her arrest and she went "underground." After six weeks on the FBI's "Most Wanted" list, she was captured. After serving 16 months in a California prison, she was acquitted of charges of kidnapping, murder, and conspiracy. During the trial, an international alliance was formed to demand her release from jail. Following her acquittal, the alliance continued to defend prison inmates, mostly black and Hispanic, against politically motivated criminal prosecutions.

After her release, Davis continued teaching, first at San Francisco State University and then at the University of California at Santa Cruz. She also teaches black female inmates in the California prison system and has written several books. She was the Vice Presidential candidate of the Communist party in 1980 and 1984.

SELECTED PUBLICATIONS
Angela Davis: An Autobiography (1974)
Women, Race, and Class (1981)
Women, Culture, and Politics (1989)

FURTHER READING
Aptheker, Bettina. *The Morning Breaks: The Trial of Angela Davis.* New York: International Publishers, 1975.
Ashman, Charles R. *The People vs. Angela Davis.* New York: Pinnacle, 1972.

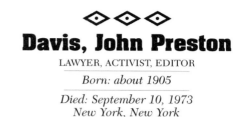

Davis, John Preston
LAWYER, ACTIVIST, EDITOR
Born: about 1905

Died: September 10, 1973
New York, New York

There is little record of Davis's life before he graduated from Bates College in Maine in 1926. After earning a law degree from Harvard in 1933, he cofounded the Joint Committee on National Recovery, an umbrella group of black organizations that worked to secure the benefits of New Deal programs for African Americans. Two years later Davis was the driving force behind the Conference on the Status of the Negro in the New Deal, held at Howard University. At that conference, Davis joined other activists and intellectuals—including Howard political scientist Ralph Bunche and the Communist party's former Vice Presidential candidate James Ford—in forming the National Negro Congress (NNC).

For the next decade, the NNC fought on many fronts, encouraging blacks to demand better wages, easier access to education, federal assistance for farmers and the unemployed, and legislation to outlaw lynching and police brutality. The NNC promoted the establishment of local communist organizations and served as a training ground for politically active African Americans who would go on to support a variety of communist initiatives and civil rights struggles.

The radical agenda of the NNC alienated much of its noncommunist membership, however. Protesting Communist party control of the NNC, its national secretary, A. Philip Randolph, resigned in 1940. Davis took his place and led the NNC until it folded in 1945. Davis then turned to publishing, editing an African-American picture magazine, *Our World*, until 1953. He edited the *American Negro Reference Book* in 1966.

FURTHER READING

Kelley, Robin. *Hammer and Hoe: Alabama Communists during the Great Depression*. Chapel Hill: University of North Carolina Press, 1990.
Klehr, Harvey. *The Heyday of American Communism: The Depression Decade*. New York: Basic Books, 1984.

Delany, Martin Robison

PHYSICIAN, PUBLICIST, AUTHOR, ACTIVIST

Born: May 6, 1812
Charles Town, Virginia (now West Virginia)

Died: January 24, 1885
Xenia, Ohio

Martin Delany was an influential abolitionist and one of the earliest and most prominent advocates of black nationalism. He popularized ideas that would later be identified with the Pan-African movement.

Delany's father, Samuel, was a slave, and his mother, Patti, was a freeperson. According to Virginia law, Martin and his siblings were born free. Because Virginia law forbade the education of black people, Martin and his family taught themselves to read and write secretly, at night. Fearing prosecution, Patti moved the children to Chambersburg, Pennsylvania, in 1822, and Samuel soon followed. In 1831 Delany moved to Pittsburgh, where he attended high school. Later he apprenticed himself

to a prominent Pittsburgh physician. He was accepted to Harvard Medical School but was forced by a protest of white students to withdraw after one semester. Delany continued his medical education elsewhere and became a prominent physician.

Between 1843 and 1847, Delany contributed to the anti-slavery efforts of Pittsburgh's African-American community by publishing an abolitionist newspaper entitled *Mystery*. Delany later moved to New York City to co-edit the *North Star* with Frederick Douglass. From his new base in New York, Delany organized antislavery meetings and lectures throughout the United States, at which he often proposed political agendas far more radical than those offered by the mainstream abolitionist movement. Delany even argued that blacks must learn "military science" so that they could defend themselves against white violence. He also demanded that supporters of emancipation invite women to participate in their conferences.

Disillusioned with the antislavery movement, in large part because white abolitionists demonstrated little concern for free blacks in the North, Delany began to explore the idea of black emigration. In 1852 he published a book in which he described blacks living in the United States as an oppressed "nation within a nation." Delany encouraged blacks to consider moving to Latin America or the West Indies. He helped form a commission to gather information on possible sites for future black settlement and made an exploratory trip to west and central Africa in 1859.

During the Civil War, President Lincoln appointed Delany the first black combat major in the Union army. After the war, he worked for the Freedmen's Bureau in Hilton Head, South Carolina, where he tried to secure land for former slaves. In 1868, he joined the Republican party and became active in South Carolina politics. But disillusioned with the party system and the failure of Reconstruction, he again supported an exodus movement in the late 1870s. In 1879, he published a book that challenged prevailing theories about black inferiority, and he argued that the origins of civilization could be traced back to black Africa.

SELECTED PUBLICATIONS

The Condition, Elevation, Emigration, and Destiny of the Colored People of the United States (1852)

Principles of Ethnology: The Origins of Races and Color (1879)

FURTHER READING

Griffith, Cyril E. *The African Dream: Martin R. Delany and the Emergence of Pan-African Thought*. University Park: Pennsylvania State University Press, 1975.

Ullman, Victor. *Martin R. Delany: The Beginnings of Black Nationalism*. Boston: Beacon, 1971.

DePriest, Oscar

POLITICIAN, BUSINESSMAN

Born: March 9, 1871
Florence, Alabama

Died: May 12, 1951
Chicago, Illinois

Oscar DePriest was the son of former slaves, both of whom were deeply involved in Reconstruction-era politics. In the late 1870s, when the federal government abandoned its commitment to protecting the voting rights of blacks, the family joined the "exoduster" migration to Kansas. DePriest moved to Chicago in 1889 and there pursued a career as a painter and decorator. He eventually built up successful businesses in construction and real estate.

In addition to his business ventures, DePriest was a hard-working organizer for the local Republican party. In 1904 he was elected to the Cook County Board of Commissioners on the Republican ticket. In 1915 he was elected Chicago's first black alderman. DePriest made a fortune in real estate during the Great Migration, profiting from black migrants' demand for housing on Chicago's South Side. As the growing black population assumed more control over local Republican party affairs, DePriest emerged as one of the most prominent and influential members of a new black leadership.

In 1928 DePriest was elected to the U.S. Congress. He was the first African American to serve in the House in 28 years and the first black from a Northern state ever to serve as a U.S. Representative. During his three terms in office, DePriest proposed—and the House consistently ignored—numerous civil rights measures, including legislation that would have outlawed lynching and government job discrimination. He fought against segregation in Washington, D.C., and helped secure funds for Howard University. As blacks switched their allegiance to the Democratic party, DePriest lost his third attempt at reelection in 1934. He returned to the real estate business and served again as alderman from 1943 to 1947.

FURTHER READING

Drake, St. Clair, and Horace R. Cayton. *Black Metropolis: A Study of Negro Life in a Northern City*. 2 vols. 1944. Reprint, New York: Harcourt, Brace, and World, 1962.

Douglass, Frederick
ABOLITIONIST, NEWSPAPER EDITOR, LECTURER

Born: February 1818
Tuckahoe, Maryland

Died: February 20, 1895
Washington, D.C.

Frederick Douglass was an ardent abolitionist, editor of antislavery newspapers, and a women's rights advocate. He was born Frederick Augustus Washington Bailey. His parents were Harriet Bailey, an enslaved woman, and an unidentified white slaveowner. Douglass was taken to Baltimore in 1826. As an urban slave, he was not as restricted as he would have been on a plantation or smaller farm. After learning how to read and write, Douglass felt that literacy opened up a new world for him. From this new form of communication, Douglass had access to information, another kind of freedom. He purchased his first book, *The Columbian Orator,* when he was in his early teens.

At the age of 18, aided by Anna Murray, a free woman from Baltimore, Douglass escaped to Massachusetts by pretending to be a free black sailor. He and Anna Murray were wed after the escape and had five children. In Massachusetts, Douglass began to lecture against slavery. He was asked to join the white-run Massachusetts Antislavery Society, an organization aligned with William Lloyd Garrison, one of the leading white abolitionists. Garrison did not advocate resistance or political action as a way to end slavery, as black abolitionists did. Douglass became a powerful lecturer on the evils of slavery, in part because he was able to speak from his own experiences.

Douglass wrote his first autobiography, *Narrative of the Life of Frederick Douglass, an American Slave, Written By Himself* in 1845. His two other narratives are *My Bondage and My Freedom* (1855) and *The Life and Times of Frederick Douglass* (1881, 1892). Because Douglass was still a fugitive, after the narrative was published he left for England to lecture against slavery. He returned to the United States in 1847 as a free man; his freedom was purchased by people he met in England.

Douglass and his family relocated to New York, where he was active in the Negro convention movement, supported woman suffrage, and edited his first antislavery newspaper, the *North Star.* By the early 1850s, Douglass was swayed by fellow abolitionists, including Henry Highland Garnet, who advocated more active abolitionism.

Douglass became active in politics, supporting the Republican party. Connecting a Union victory with an end to slavery, he urged African-American men to fight for the Union army. Two of Frederick Douglass's sons, Charles and Lewis, served with the 54th Regiment. After the Civil War, Douglass moved to Washington, D.C., where he held a number of government appointments.

Douglass's life stands as a powerful symbol of the transformation of African Americans from enslavement to freedom.

FURTHER READING
Douglass, Frederick. *The Oxford Frederick Douglass Reader.* Edited by William L. Andrews. New York: Oxford University Press, 1996.
Huggins, Nathan Irvin. *Slave and Citizen: The Life of Frederick Douglass.* Boston: Little, Brown, 1980.

McFeely, William S. *Frederick Douglass*. New York: Norton, 1991.

Russell, Sharman Apt. *Frederick Douglass.* New York: Chelsea House, 1988.

Voss, Frederick. *Majestic in his Wrath: A Pictorial Life of Frederick Douglass.* Washington, D.C. : Smithsonian Institution Press, 1995.

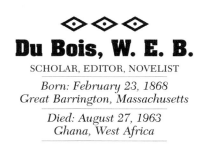

Du Bois, W. E. B.

SCHOLAR, EDITOR, NOVELIST

Born: February 23, 1868
Great Barrington, Massachusetts

Died: August 27, 1963
Ghana, West Africa

William Edward Burghardt Du Bois was one of the foremost intellectuals of the 20th century. Much of our thinking about race comes from his writings. Often contrasted with Booker T. Washington, who emphasized economics and industrial education, Du Bois advocated a liberal arts education and political action as the foundation for black progress. Du Bois, the editor of the NAACP's magazine, *The Crisis,* author of 16 books, 2 autobiographies, 5 works of fiction, hundreds of articles, and a leader in the Pan-African movement, led a long and productive life. At the time of his death, Du Bois was still searching for answers and continued to wonder whether blacks could achieve justice in the United States.

Du Bois earned his first B.A. in 1888 from Fisk University in Nashville, Tennessee. He then went to Harvard University, where he earned another B.A. (1890) and a Ph.D. in history (1895). During his doctoral studies at Harvard, he spent two years at the University of Berlin studying history, sociology, and philosophy.

After Harvard, Du Bois taught at Wilberforce University in Ohio for two years. He left Wilberforce to conduct a commissioned sociological study of blacks in Philadelphia, which was published as *The Philadelphia Negro* (1899). After that project was completed he went to Atlanta University to teach and do research.

Du Bois organized the Niagara Movement, the forerunner to the National Association for the Advancement of Colored People (NAACP), in 1905. Many of the people involved with the short-lived Niagara Movement later joined the NAACP when it was created in 1909. The NAACP, an interracial organization of men and women, was founded in response to the 1908 Springfield, Illinois, race riot. Du Bois joined the NAACP as director of research and began publishing *The Crisis: A Record of the Darker Races,* a monthly magazine that started in November 1910 (*The Crisis* is still being published). In the pages of *The Crisis,* Du Bois advanced his own ideas, and also published poems, NAACP news, bibliographies, and articles featuring different aspects of black life in the United States and abroad.

Politically, Du Bois started out as an integrationist, pushing for full citizenship rights and inclusion. By World War II, Du Bois had moved further to the left, toward socialism. He became more firmly convinced that black struggles in the United States had to be joined with anticapitalist and Third World struggles. In the late 1940s, he worked with Paul Robeson, Max Yergan, and Alphaeus Hunton on the Council on African Affairs, a Pan-

Africanist organization that served as a clearinghouse of information on Africa as well as a lobbying group. In 1961 Du Bois became a member of the Communist party.

Du Bois's final project was an encyclopedia of the African diaspora—*Encyclopedia Africana*. He began the research for this work in Ghana, his new home.

SELECTED PUBLICATIONS
The Souls of Black Folk (1903)
The Quest of the Silver Fleece: A Novel (1911)
*Dusk of Dawn: An Essay toward an
    Autobiography of a Race Concept* (1940)
The World and Africa (1946)
Black Reconstruction in America (1935)

FURTHER READING
Lewis, David Levering. *W. E. B. Du Bois: The Biography of a Race*. New York: Holt, 1993.
Stafford, Mark. *W. E. B. Du Bois*. New York: Chelsea House, 1989.
Sundquist, Eric, ed. *The Oxford W. E. B. Du Bois Reader*. New York: Oxford University Press, 1996.

Ellington, Edward Kennedy "Duke"

COMPOSER, PIANIST, BANDLEADER

*Born: April 29, 1899
Washington, D.C.*

*Died: May 24, 1974
New York, New York*

Duke Ellington, a composer of jazz, spirituals, classical music, and ballads, created more than 3,000 compositions. Known worldwide for his musical genius, Ellington stands out as an innovator who collaborated with other musicians, artists, and dancers. One of his most meaningful collaborations was with composer Billy Strayhorn, who composed many famous jazz standards, including *Take the A Train*. Duke Ellington once wrote, "I think of myself as a messenger boy. And I want all the help I can get . . . to say what I hope I am good enough to say."

Born to parents who had studied piano, Ellington began learning music at the age of six. He grew up in Washington, D.C., which in the early 1920s was home to a number of popular clubs where local and touring performers would play. Ellington learned much of his style from listening to the bands in these clubs. By the time he was 16, he had written his first song, "Soda Fountain Rag." In spite of his obvious talent for music, Ellington's first artistic interests were drawing and painting. He even won a scholarship to Pratt Institute in Brooklyn, New York, but decided to pursue music instead.

Ellington left high school and started his own band before he was 20. In 1923 he moved to New York with the Washingtonians, a band led by Elmer Snowden. New York, New Orleans, Chicago, and Kansas City were the hottest cities for jazz, each giving birth to distinct styles. In the 1920s, New York musicians were playing mainly big band jazz. Big bands usually consisted of a large brass and reed section, as well as a piano, bass, and drum player.

Ellington replaced Snowden as leader of the Washingtonians in 1924. He continued to compose songs and was able to get consistent gigs for the band. In 1927 the band began playing at the Cotton Club, one of Harlem's most popular nightspots. (Harlem's black residents were not welcome then, however; it was an all-white club until 1928.) The Cotton Club performances were broadcast over national radio, making his music accessible to a larger audience.

As swing declined in importance by the 1940s, Ellington took his band on tours abroad. He also began to break out of his focus on jazz compositions and write gospel music as well as compose music for film and dance concerts.

PUBLICATION
Music Is My Mistress (1973)

FURTHER READING
Frankl, Ron. *Duke Ellington.* New York: Chelsea House, 1988.
Hasse, John Edward. *Beyond Category: The Life and Genius of Duke Ellington.* New York: Simon & Schuster, 1993.
Tucker, Mark, ed. *The Duke Ellington Reader.* New York: Oxford University Press, 1993.

Ellison, Ralph
WRITER

Born: March 1, 1914
Oklahoma City, Oklahoma

Died: April 16, 1994
New York, New York

"I am an invisible man. I am invisible, understand, simply because people refuse to see me." These are some of the first lines in Ralph Ellison's novel, *Invisible Man,* for which he won the National Book Award in 1952. Ellison had a prolific career as a fiction writer and cultural critic. In his nonfiction essays on black culture—music, dance, and visual arts—Ellison explored the beauty and intelligence of these expressions and insisted on their importance in the development of American culture.

In high school in Oklahoma City, Ellison played in several jazz bands and was a member of the varsity football team. In 1933 he received a scholarship from the state of Oklahoma to attend Tuskegee Institute in Alabama, where he majored in music. After three years, he decided to relocate to New York to study sculpture and music composition.

Ellison's first published work was a review for *New Challenge,* a magazine edited by writer Richard Wright, who became Ellison's friend and mentor. Ellison would continue to write book reviews, short stories, and sketches for a number of journals. It was often difficult to earn a living as a writer in the 1930s. Many authors held odd jobs to supplement their income. Others had patrons—usually white—who supported them financially. During the Great Depression, President Roosevelt instituted a number of New Deal programs promoting art and recreation. Ellison worked for one of these programs—the Works Progress Administration's (WPA) New York Writers Project. For one of the WPA's folklore projects, he collected stories from hundreds of families living in New York City apartments.

Invisible Man is Ellison's major work and his only published novel. Set between 1930 and 1950, it is a classic tale about a young man's quest for identity. The central character is a black man from the South who goes to college and then to New York. The hero experiences white racism, alienation from other blacks, and struggles with adaptation to Harlem, the prototypical northern urban center.

In 1955 Ellison was awarded the Prix de Rome by the American Academy of Arts and

Letters, which enabled him to live and write in Italy. In 1964 Ellison published *Shadow and Act,* a collection of essays on U.S. culture. He completed another collection of essays, *Going to the Territory*, in 1986. When Ellison died in 1994, he was working on another novel.

PUBLICATIONS
Invisible Man (1952)
Shadow and Act (1964)
Going to the Territory (1986)

FURTHER READING
Bishop, Jack. *Ralph Ellison.* New York: Chelsea House, 1988.
O'Meally, Robert G. *The Craft of Ralph Ellison.* Cambridge, Mass.: Harvard University Press, 1980.

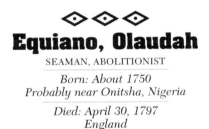

Equiano, Olaudah

SEAMAN, ABOLITIONIST

Born: About 1750
Probably near Onitsha, Nigeria

Died: April 30, 1797
England

Olaudah Equiano was born in Benin, the son of an Ibo chieftain. When he was 11 years old, Equiano and his sister were kidnapped by enemies of their tribe. He was eventually separated from his sister and sold to white slave traders on the West African coast. Surviving the Middle Passage, Equiano was eventually bought by a British naval officer named Pascal, who gave him the name Gustavas Vassa. During his 17 years serving Pascal, Equiano sailed the Atlantic and lived in England. He learned to read and write and was forcibly converted to Christianity. Purchased next by an American shipowner, Equiano worked on a vessel that made trade runs between the West Indies and North America. The cargo often included enslaved blacks.

Equiano purchased his freedom in 1766 and spent the next several years continuing to work as a seaman. By the late 1770s, he was spending most of his time in the British Isles, where he took an active role in the antislavery movement. In 1789 he published his autobiography, *The Interesting Narrative of Olaudah Equiano, or Gustavus Vassa the African, written by himself*. In this book, Equiano described his life in Africa before enslavement, the experience of the Middle Passage, and his life as a slave in the British West Indies, North America, and England. He documented the horrors and inhumanity of the institution of slavery and called for its abolition. Equiano intended for his work to spark debate; he sent copies of the autobiography directly to members of the British Parliament who were debating the future of the nation's participation in the slave trade.

Equiano's *Narrative* attracted a wide readership and went through nine printings in Great Britain within a decade of its publication. Equiano was invited to lecture on slavery throughout the British Isles. Two years after it was published in England, the autobiography appeared in the United States, and Dutch and German translations followed. Equiano's narrative also had an enduring impact on the tradition of black autobiographical writing. His account influenced the ways that African Americans later described their experiences in the "slave narratives" of the 19th century.

PUBLICATION
The Interesting Narrative of Olaudah Equiano, or Gustavus Vassa the African, written by himself (1789, reprint 1995)

Farmer, James

CIVIL RIGHTS LEADER, EDUCATOR

Born: January 12, 1920
Marshall, Texas

James Farmer's mother was a homemaker and former teacher, and his father was a Methodist minister and scholar. The family moved several times when Farmer was young so that his father could accept a series of academic positions. James attended school first in Holly Springs, Mississippi, then in Austin, Texas, and finally in Atlanta.

At age 14 Farmer entered Wiley College in Marshall, Texas, where he was captain of the debate team and active in Methodist youth groups. He then studied theology at Howard University, where Howard Thurman, a black professor of social ethics, introduced him to the work of Mahatma Gandhi, the Indian pacifist and activist. Thurman was also vice-chairman of a national pacifist organization, the Fellowship of Reconciliation (FOR), and arranged a part-time job for Farmer as a FOR student secretary in Washington, D.C.

Upon graduation from Howard in 1941, Farmer accepted a position in Chicago as race-relations secretary with FOR. Working with other young activists, many of whom were FOR members, Farmer drew up a plan for an interracial civil rights organization that would be dedicated to nonviolent, direct action, on the model of Gandhi's writings and political protests. Early in 1942, Farmer and his colleagues tested some of Gandhi's methods by initiating protests against a local diner and skating rink that discriminated against black people. That spring, with the momentum of these early efforts behind them, Farmer and five other young activists—one of them black, four of them white—founded the Congress of Racial Equality (CORE).

Nonviolent, direct action protests had been employed before, but Farmer and his colleagues were the first to outline a theory and a systematic strategy for using nonviolent protest in the fight against racial discrimination in the U.S. Farmer served as the director of CORE in its early years, as dedicated activists—mostly young, well-educated, and middle class—opened independent chapters in several Northern and Western cities. He resigned as director in 1946 to work as a labor organizer and later as a staff member for the NAACP. Yet Farmer still participated in CORE activities in the late 1940s and 1950s, as dozens of CORE chapters—including new chapters in the South—organized sit-ins and other actions to combat the segregation of public facilities, jobs and housing.

CORE's activities received little media attention until direct, nonviolent action became a prominent tool of the civil rights movement in the late 1950s. Following the wave of student-led sit-ins and arrests in early 1960, CORE's national office invited Farmer to replace James Robinson as the organization's leader. In 1961 Farmer organized the Freedom Rides, in which black and white activists challenged the segregation of interstate buses and bus terminals, facing violence and arrest. (In 1947, sixteen members of CORE and FOR had staged a similar, if less ambitious campaign to integrate buses.) Farmer was one of 360 activists, including leaders of CORE, SNCC, and SCLC, who were arrested and jailed during the Freedom Rides.

With nonviolent protest now in the media spotlight, the charismatic Farmer helped bring national attention and recognition to CORE. As the organization gained more members and resources, chapters in Northern cities focused on campaigns against discrimination in housing and employment, while Southern chapters concentrated on voter registration drives. The composition of CORE's membership began to change as well, as more and more African Americans, many of them working class, joined an organization that had traditionally been mostly white and middle class. Throughout these years, Farmer stressed the links between racial and economic discrimination in the U.S., arguing that the government should intervene to ensure that African Americans had equal access to education, job training, and employment. Through his activism, public lectures, and writings on nonviolent protest, Farmer emerged as one of the most prominent leaders of the civil rights movement.

Farmer left CORE in 1966, as the organization abandoned its commitment to interracial and nonviolent strategies. After teaching at Lincoln University in Pennsylvania and losing a campaign for Congress in 1968, Farmer accepted a position in Richard Nixon's administration as Assistant Secretary of Health, Education and Welfare. After resigning the post in 1971, he spent the next decade sponsoring and working for a number of nonprofit organizations that addressed civil rights, labor, and housing issues. Since 1982, Farmer has taught at Mary Washington College in Fredericksburg, Virginia.

PUBLICATIONS
Freedom—When? (1965)
Lay Bare the Heart: An Autobiography of the Civil Rights Movement (1985)

FURTHER READING
Meier, August, and Elliott Rudwick. *CORE: A Study in the Civil Rights Movement, 1942–1968.* New York: Oxford University Press, 1973.
Sklansky, Jeff. *James Farmer.* New York: Chelsea House, 1991.

Farrakhan, Louis (Louis Eugene Walcott)

ISLAMIC MINISTER, POLITICAL LEADER

*Born: May 11, 1933
New York, New York*

Louis Farrakhan, national representative of the Nation of Islam, has been involved in black nationalist politics since the early 1960s. Although many citizens were not introduced to Farrakhan until his televised speech at the Million Man March, held on October 16, 1995, Farrakhan has enjoyed a large following nationwide as a charismatic speaker for over 20 years.

Born Louis Eugene Walcott and raised Episcopalian, Louis Farrakhan studied the violin and piano in his youth. He attended Winston-Salem Teachers College in North Carolina in the early 1950s and eventually moved to Boston, where he performed as Calypso Gene, often incorporating political themes in his songs. He was recruited into the Nation of Islam in 1955 and became leader of the Boston mosque in the early 1960s. Farrakhan replaced Malcolm X as head of the Harlem Mosque after Malcolm X left the Nation of Islam in 1964.

After the death of Nation of Islam founder Elijah Muhammad in 1975, his son Wallace D. Muhammad renamed the organization, rejecting his father's black nationalist philosophy. Dissatisfied with Wallace D. Muhammad's new organization, Farrakhan declared himself leader of the Nation of Islam three years later. Farrakhan espoused most of the doctrine laid out by Muhammad—the importance of a self-sufficient black nation within the United States in which economic development and self-knowledge were key. Unlike Muhammad, however, Farrakhan advocated participation in electoral politics. Farrakhan supported Jesse Jackson's campaign for the Presidency in 1984 and in 1988. In addition, Nation of Islam members worked on behalf of local and congressional candidates in 1990.

Farrakhan is revered by members of the Nation of Islam and by those who attend his lectures because he is seen as one of the few leaders who speaks openly about white supremacy and because he operates from an all-black, self-supporting organization. Farrakhan is also widely criticized for advocating black separatism, for making anti-Semitic remarks, and for his conservatism on issues of gender and the role of the federal government in the welfare of African Americans. In 1996, Farrakhan went on a continent-wide tour of Africa, meeting with leaders, in part, to raise money for projects in the United States.

PUBLICATIONS
Seven Speeches by Minister Louis Farrakhan (1974)
A Torchlight for America (1993)

FURTHER READING
Eure, Joseph D., and Richard M. Jerome, eds. *Back Where We Belong: Selected Speeches by Minister Louis Farrakhan.* Philadelphia: P. C. International Press, 1989.
Haskins, Jim. *Louis Farrakhan and the Nation of Islam.* New York: Walker and Co., 1996.
Magida, Arthur J. *Prophet of Rage: A Life of Louis Farrakhan and His Nation.* New York: Basic, 1996.
Reed, Jr. Adolph. "The Rise of Louis Farrakhan." *The Nation* (January 28, 1991), 1, 51–55.
———. "All for One and None for All." *The Nation* (January 28, 1991), 86–92.

Fauset, Jessie Redmon
AUTHOR, EDITOR, TEACHER

Born: April 26, 1882
Fredericksville, New Jersey

Died: April 30, 1961
Philadelphia, Pennsylvania

Jessie Fauset was raised in Philadelphia by her widowed father, who was an African Methodist Episcopal minister. After graduating Phi Beta Kappa from Cornell University in 1905, Fauset taught high school French in Washington, D.C., while earning a master's degree from the University of Pennsylvania. Beginning in 1919, Fauset served as a literary editor and author for *The Crisis*, the magazine of the National Association of Colored People.

By publishing early work by writers such as Arna Bontemps, Langston Hughes, Anne Spencer, George Schuyler, and Jean Toomer in *The Crisis*, Fauset helped introduce some of the most influential writers of the Harlem Renaissance. Committed to supporting black writers, and convinced that African-American art was a critical component of blacks' struggle for equality, Fauset helped make *The Crisis* an important venue for the new literary modernism of the 1920s. She wrote for the journal as well, contributing biographical sketches, travel accounts, reviews, and reports on black political issues and black women activists. She also reviewed and translated the work of French-speaking authors from Africa and the Caribbean. In 1921, she helped W. E. B. Du Bois develop a monthly magazine for children, *The Brownies' Book*, and served as its literary editor.

Fauset published several novels, including *There Is Confusion* (1924) and *Plum Bun* (1929). Her fiction chronicled the condition of African Americans, especially women, and it explored complicated questions about racial and gender identity. Many of her contemporaries and later critics, however, accused her of proposing sentimental solutions to the problems that blacks faced in the United States.

In 1926 Fauset retired from *The Crisis*. Despite her education, skills, and experience, she was unable to find work in the segregated world of New York publishing. The following year she returned to teaching and removed herself from public life. She published two more novels, *The Chinaberry Tree* (1931) and *Comedy: American Style* (1933).

SELECTED PUBLICATIONS
Plum Bun (1929)
The Chinaberry Tree (1931)

FURTHER READING
Johnson-Feelings, Dianne, ed. *The Best of The Brownies' Book*. New York: Oxford University Press, 1995.
Lewis, David Levering. *When Harlem Was in Vogue*. New York: Knopf, 1981.
Sylvander, Carolyn. *Jessie Redmon Fauset: Black American Writer.* Troy, N.Y.: Whitson, 1981.
Wall, Cheryl A. *Women of the Harlem Renaissance*. Bloomington: Indiana University Press, 1995.

◇ ◇ ◇
Fisher, Rudolph
WRITER, SCIENTIST
Born: May 9, 1897
Washington, D.C.

Died: December 26, 1934
New York, New York

Rudolph Fisher was a scientist, novelist, and short story writer. In his brief life, he co-authored two scientific articles, had 15 of his short stories published, and wrote two novels and a play. In addition to researching and writing in the fields of science and literature, Fisher played the piano and wrote musical scores. Although not as well known as other Harlem Renaissance writers, Fisher hoped to be remembered as an interpreter of Harlem life.

Fisher grew up in Providence, Rhode Island. He excelled academically in high school, then attended Brown University, where he was also a stellar student, combining his interests in biology and English. He was elected to the Phi Beta Kappa national honor society, and was also the commencement speaker at his graduation in 1919. After receiving his A.M. degree the following year, also from Brown, he entered Howard University Medical School, graduating in 1925.

Fisher's ability to use all of his talents simultaneously was evident during his college years. During the summer after his college graduation, he and Paul Robeson combined their musical talents—Robeson as singer and Fisher as pianist and arranger—and toured along the East coast. During his last year in medical school, Fisher started writing "The City of Refuge," his first published story.

After graduating from medical school, Fisher and his wife, Jane Ryder, and their newborn baby moved to New York City, where he began his research at Columbia University on ultraviolet rays and viruses, with financial support from a National Research Council fellowship. By 1930 Fisher had opened a private practice in Harlem; later he moved to Long Island.

Fisher was one of the few Harlem Renaissance writers who actually wrote about Harlem. By the 1920s Harlem was considered the black cultural capital in the United States. Fisher tried to capture its complexity in his work. He frequented dance halls and jazz clubs as a way of "researching" his stories and novels. His second novel, *The Conjure Man Dies*, was one of the earliest black detective novels published. Fisher predates Chester Himes, who wrote the first of his nine detective novels in 1958, and Ishmael Reed, who began writing in the 1960s.

Fisher died at 37 after undergoing surgery for a stomach disorder.

SELECTED PUBLICATIONS
The Walls of Jericho (1928)
The Conjure Man Dies (1932)
The City of Refuge: The Collected Stories of Rudolph Fisher. Edited by John McCluskey, Jr. Columbia: University of Missouri Press, 1987.

Foster, Andrew "Rube"
BASEBALL PITCHER AND MANAGER
Born: September 17, 1879
Calvert, Texas

Died: December 9, 1930
Kankakee, Illinois

Andrew Foster, elected to the Baseball Hall of Fame in 1981, was an outstanding pitcher, manager, and promoter of baseball. Foster began his baseball career with a local team, the Waco Yellow Jackets. He moved on to a Chicago team, the Leland Giants. He also played briefly for a white, semiprofessional team in Michigan. In 1903 he joined the Cuban X-Giants, a Philadelphia team, considered the best team in the East. (The use of the term "Cuban" dates back to the 1880s, to the Cuban Giants of New York. Many black players believed that they would experience less racism if whites thought they were Cuban.) Foster also formed a team called the Chicago American Giants, whose members included John Henry Lloyd and Grant "Home Run" Johnson.

In 1920 Foster met with the owners of six black teams to discuss the formation of a professional league. In the decade before, Foster had served as a booking agent for semiprofessional teams in Chicago. He often found it difficult to book games, particularly on the East Coast, because of the virtual monopoly held by white booking agent Nat Strong. Although two previous attempts to form black leagues—the International League of Independent Baseball Clubs (1906) and the National Negro Baseball League (1910)—had failed, Foster felt that a new league would enable him and other promoters to get around Strong. The National Association of Professional Baseball Clubs, consisting of six teams in midwestern cities, was founded in Kansas City in 1920. Foster was elected president and treasurer of the league, commonly known as the Negro National League. In 1923 Nat Strong founded the Eastern Colored League. The champions of the two leagues competed in a World Series.

The Negro National League offered athletes an opportunity to play the sport that they loved and excelled in, and provided a popular source of entertainment for spectators.

FURTHER READING
Margolies, Jacob. *The Negro League: The Story of Black Baseball.* New York: Watts, 1993.
Peterson, Robert. *Only the Ball Was White.* New Jersey: McGraw-Hill, 1970.

Franklin, Aretha
SINGER

Born: March 25, 1942
Memphis, Tennessee

The "Queen of Soul," as Aretha Franklin would be crowned in the mid-1960s, grew up in Detroit. As a child she sang in the choir at New Bethel Baptist Church, where her father was the pastor. Her father had a tremendous influence on her singing, as did Clara Ward, Mahalia Jackson, and other gospel artists who visited the Franklin home. Aretha sang in a gospel quartet with her sister Emma and traveled the midwestern gospel circuit with her father where she sang with the region's greatest artists. At 14 she made a recording of gospel songs.

Four years later, in 1960, she signed with Columbia Records to make an album of secular music. The producers at Columbia did not appreciate Franklin's unique interpretations of popular songs, so in 1966 she switched to Atlantic Records, where she was encouraged to record arrangements that acknowledged her background as a gospel and rhythm and blues artist. Her early recordings on Atlantic were instant hits that helped change the face of popular music. In songs such as "I Never Loved A Man (The Way I Love You)," "Respect," and "(You Make Me Feel Like) A Natural Woman," Franklin continued to introduce a broad national audience to the emotional power of black music.

Since her breakthrough in 1967, Franklin has recorded 35 records and received 15 Grammy awards, 3 American Music awards, and a Grammy Living Legend award. Seventeen of her singles have topped the R&B charts. In the 1970s Franklin experimented with a variety of musical styles and her recordings were far less popular. She then made a commercial comeback in the 1980s, most notably with her 1985 recording *Who's Zoomin' Who* and in collaborations with contemporary pop artists.

FURTHER READING
Bego, Mark. *Aretha Franklin: Queen of Soul.* New York: St. Martin's, 1989.
Shaw, Arnold. *Black Popular Music in America: From the Spirituals, Minstrels, and Ragtime to Soul, Disco, and Hip-Hop.* New York: Schirmer, 1986.

Frazier, E. Franklin
SOCIOLOGIST, ACTIVIST

Born: September 24, 1894
Baltimore, Maryland

Died: May 17, 1962
Washington, D.C.

E. Franklin Frazier devoted his professional career to researching and writing about African Americans. Through his eight books, more than 100 articles, and lectures to church clubs, women's organizations, farmers' coopera-tives, unions, and Pan-African organizations, Frazier helped—along with other sociologists of his generation—Horace Cayton, St. Clair Drake, and Ira de A. Reid—to shape the ways in which African Americans were perceived and written about. He was particularly concerned with the impact of enslavement and urbaniza-tion on individuals, families, and institutions.

Frazier grew up in a working-class family in Baltimore. His father had a strong sense of race pride and gave Frazier and his siblings newspaper clippings on blacks worldwide. Frazier used to tell the story of how he would spit at the Johns Hopkins University buildings as a young person because of Hopkins's whites-only admissions policy.

Frazier received his undergraduate degree from Howard University in 1916 and earned a Ph.D in sociology from the University of Chicago in 1931. He served as professor and chair of the sociology department at Howard from 1934 to 1959, helping to turn the univer-sity into a major research center.

In addition to his scholarly excellence, Frazier was outspoken about racism. In June 1927, he wrote an article in *The Forum* in which he argued that certain symptoms of white racial prejudice were no different from the symptoms of insanity. Frazier was also out-spoken about what he considered to be Negro cowardice. When Juliette Derricotte, dean of women at Fisk University, lost her life because a white hospital refused to treat her after a car accident, Frazier wrote letters to the press and discussed the incident with his classes, even though the president of Fisk ordered faculty to refrain from speaking about it. Frazier was also

a non-conformist in religion. He was an avowed atheist. Despite his extensive research on the role of churches in black life, religion had no place in his personal life.

The first entry in Frazier's 1950 diary states, "A diary is especially necessary at this time when the Fascist-minded men who are going to preserve American 'democracy' are prepar-ing padlocks first for the mouths of the teach-ers." Frazier wrote this at the beginning of the Cold War, when perceived anti-Americanism could result in being fired and worse. He had long been aware that speaking out—whether in a university classroom, a book, or a speech—was often dangerous but necessary.

SELECTED PUBLICATIONS
Negro Youth at the Crossways: Their Personality Development in the Middle States (1940, reprint 1968)
The Negro in the United States (1949)
Black Bourgeoisie (1957)
The Negro Church in America (1963)

FURTHER READING
Platt, Anthony M. *E. Franklin Frazier Reconsidered*. New Brunswick, N.J.: Rutgers University Press, 1991.

Garnet, Henry Highland

RELIGIOUS LEADER, ABOLITIONIST

Born: December 23, 1815
Kent County, Maryland

Died: February 14, 1882
Monrovia, Liberia

"Brethren, arise, arise! Strike for your lives and liberties. Let every slave throughout the land do this and the days of slavery are numbered. Awake, Awake, no oppressed people have secured their liberty without resistance." These incendiary words were part of a speech entitled "Address to the Slaves of the United States of America" that Henry Highland Garnet gave at a Buffalo convention in 1843. Garnet lived a full life fighting against slavery, doing missionary work, and serving as pastor of numerous churches.

Garnet was born enslaved. His family was able to escape to New York City, becoming free people, when he was nine years old. This act of freeing one's self was the first step in a long career of abolitionist work. Garnet's early life was shaped by Theodore S. Wright and Peter Williams, Jr., who ran the school he attended, the Canal Street High School. Wright and Williams were important religious leaders and active abolitionists as well as educators. After graduation, Garnet attended the predominantly white Noyes Academy in New Hampshire, then transferred to Oneida Institute in Whitesboro, New York, graduating in 1839. As a pastor at the Liberty Street Presbyterian Church in Troy, New York, beginning in 1840, Garnet opened the church as a safe place for runaway slaves and edited two antislavery newspapers.

In addition to his abolitionist work, Garnet was a leader in the Pan-Africanist movement. As the first president of the African Colonization Society (ACS), he sought to establish connections between blacks in the United States and continental Africans. One of the ACS's goals was to send selected American blacks to West Africa with the hope of turning the Africans into Christians. Garnet also hoped that establishing cotton fields in Africa would cause cotton prices to fall, thereby hastening the end of slavery in the United States. Because of financial difficulties as well as its

association with white-run colonization societies, the ACS realized few of its goals under Garnet's leadership.

Garnet was able to realize his dream of living in Africa when he accepted a position as U.S. minister to Liberia in 1881.

FURTHER READING
Schor, Joel. *Henry Highland Garnet: A Voice of Black Radicalism in the Nineteenth Century*. Westport, Conn.: Greenwood, 1977.

◇ ◇ ◇
Garvey, Marcus Mosiah
PAN-AFRICANIST

Born: August 7, 1887
St. Ann's Bay, Jamaica

Died: June 10, 1940
London, England

Marcus Garvey was active in working-class politics in Jamaica as a young man. He participated in a printers' union strike while he was an apprentice. From that experience, as well as his travels throughout Central America and London, where he met pan-Africanist Duse Mohamed Ali, Garvey witnessed how people of African descent were similarly oppressed despite their location.

He returned to Jamaica and in 1914 founded the Universal Negro Improvement Association–African Communities League (UNIA–ACL). It became an international organization with branches in Africa, Central and South America, Europe, Canada, and the United States. Blacks joined the organization in great numbers, making it the largest black movement ever. Garvey's philosophy of black pride, self-reliance, entrepreneurship, and nationhood fit well with the concept of the New Negro after World War I.

Garvey emigrated to the United States in 1916 and a year later started the first U.S. branch in Harlem. Garvey, apparently influenced by World War I, believed that the future of the black diaspora rested on a unified, free Africa. Africa had been divided up by European powers in the late 19th century and remained under colonial rule.

One of Garvey's major projects was the creation of the Black Star Steamship Corporation in 1919. The Black Star Line would ship people and products between the different continents, forming the beginning of a black economic base. Garvey offered blacks the opportunity to purchase shares in the company. Although the project ultimately failed, it was a tremendous source of pride and hope.

Garvey was much more successful in other efforts. With the financial support of Madam C. J. Walker and others, he was able to purchase a building in New York, which he named Liberty Hall and where he held annual conventions of the UNIA. Garvey also published a weekly newspaper, *Negro World*, which kept members throughout the diaspora abreast of UNIA activities.

Though Garvey was loved by his members, he had numerous adversaries, including the federal government and other black leaders. Garvey was convicted of mail fraud and deported to Jamaica in 1927. He attempted unsuccessfully to revive the UNIA in Jamaica. In 1935 he moved to London, where he remained active until his death in 1940. The UNIA continues as an organization today.

FURTHER READING
Garvey, Amy Jacques. *The Philosophy and Opinions of Marcus Garvey*, with an Introduction by Robert A. Hill. New York: Atheneum, 1992.
Lawler, Mary. *Marcus Garvey*. New York: Chelsea House, 1988.
Martin, Tony. *Literary Garveyism: Garveyism, Black Arts, and the Harlem Renaissance*. Dover, Mass.: Majority Press, 1983.

Grace, Charles M. "Sweet Daddy"

RELIGIOUS LEADER, BUSINESSMAN

Born: January 25, 1881
Brava, Cape Verde Islands

Died: January 12, 1960
Los Angeles, California

Daddy Grace, founder of the United House of Prayer for All People, Church on the Rock of the Apostolic Faith, built a major religious following that continues today. Starting from a small mission in Massachusetts, Daddy Grace amassed an estate worth $25 million, with an estimated 3 million followers in 350 churches across cities throughout the United States. One of a number of Pentecostal leaders who surfaced during the Depression, Grace offered religious seekers an alternative to traditional Protestantism.

Grace was born Marceline Manoel de Graca on the Cape Verde Islands, located off the coast of West Africa. He emigrated to the United States in the early 1900s and began working as a cranberry picker. It appears that he began preaching at a young age, spreading his message from a maroon Studebaker. After a visit to the Holy Land he was determined to build a church.

Grace, after establishing his first missions in Massachusetts, chose Washington, D.C., as the headquarters for his church in 1926 and moved to the District of Columbia one year later. The nation's capital was also home to Elder Lightfoot Solomon Michaux's Church of God. Michaux, known as the "Happy Am I Evangelist," broadcast sermons over the radio and shared his message in his *Happy Am I News* newspaper.

Grace's theology was based on the teachings of Jesus Christ and the Old Testament. In addition, Grace believed in the power of the Holy Ghost; he and his followers would sometimes "speak in tongues" as a result of getting the spirit. Grace gained many of his followers from the revivals and mass baptisms he offered throughout the country. Grace, who was charismatic and had his own unique style, led an opulent life. Fond of green and purple coats with gold trimmings, Grace had long fingernails which he painted red, white, and blue, and also wore his hair long. From the money donated by his followers, he acquired hotels, apartment buildings, restaurants, and beauty parlors. Grace also had a fruit farm in Cuba and a coffee plantation in Brazil.

Grace died during one of his frequent trips to Los Angeles. He was prepared for his own death; he tape recorded the eulogy that was played during his funeral.

FURTHER READING

Davis, Lenwood G. *Daddy Grace: An Annotated Bibliography*. New York: Greenwood, 1992.
Fauset, Arthur Huff. *Black Gods of the Metropolis: Negro Religious Cults of the Urban North*. Philadelphia: University of Pennsylvania Press, 1944.

Haley, Alex

WRITER, LECTURER, GENEALOGY CONSULTANT

Born: August 11, 1921
Ithaca, New York

Died: February 10, 1992
Seattle, Washington

Born in upstate New York, Alex Haley spent summers in Henning, Tennessee, with his mother's family. He graduated from high school at 15 and spent two years in college before joining the U.S. Coast Guard in 1939. Haley perfected his writing skills while in the Coast Guard. His first published stories were adventures. Eventually the Coast Guard promoted him to the position of chief journalist.

In 1959 he retired from the Coast Guard with hopes of living on his earnings as a writer. His hopes were realized after an interview with Miles Davis for *Playboy* magazine in 1962. In that same year he interviewed Malcolm X for *Playboy,* which led to a collaboration with Malcolm X on his autobiography.

In 1965 Haley began the research for *Roots.* He started with his grandmother's oral history of her family, snippets of which he had heard during his summers in Henning. She told him about the "furthest-back person"—a slave named Toby. His intensive search through archives and libraries in the United States, Africa, and Europe led him to a village on the Gambia River in West Africa, where the Kinte clan resided. *Roots* follows Toby (Kunta Kinte) from his capture by white slavers in West Africa to his enslavement and emancipation in the U.S. South.

After *Roots* was published and made into a television mini-series, Haley was catapulted into fame and found himself in demand for lectures and interviews. He and his brother started a foundation for the study of black genealogy. Before his death in 1992, Haley was working on a biography of his grandmother and a history of Henning.

PUBLICATIONS
The Autobiography of Malcolm X (with Malcolm X, 1965)
Roots (1976)
Alex Haley's Queen: The Story of an American Family (with David Stevens, 1993)

FURTHER READING
Gonzales, Doreen. *Alex Haley: Author of Roots.* Englewood Cliffs, N.J.: Enslow, 1994.
Shirley, David. *Alex Haley.* New York: Chelsea House, 1994.
Wolper, David L., with Quincy Troupe. *The Inside Story of TV's "Roots."* New York: Warner, 1978.

Hamer, Fannie Lou

ACTIVIST

Born: October 6, 1917
Montgomery County, Mississippi

Died: March 14, 1977
Mound Bayou, Mississippi

The youngest of 20 children born to Jim and Lou Ella Townsend, Fannie Lou Hamer began working at age six. Like so many poor blacks living in the South at the time, she grew up chopping and picking cotton. Because she could read and write, a local plantation owner hired her as a record keeper in 1944. She married that same year and set up a house in Ruleville, Mississippi—where the couple raised two adopted daughters—and worked as a sharecropper and record keeper until 1962.

That year at a mass meeting organized by the Student Nonviolent Coordinating Committee (SNCC), Hamer volunteered to go to the local courthouse to register to vote. She and 17 others were arrested. That night the owner of the plantation on which she worked forced her to leave; days later local whites shot at the house in which Hamer had sought refuge.

She devoted the rest of her life to political organizing. Hamer worked with the SNCC chapter in Ruleville and within a year became a SNCC field secretary. In 1964 she joined local activists in founding the Mississippi Freedom Democratic Party (MFDP). She then helped to register the 63,000 blacks who supported the MFDP's challenge to the all-white state delegation at the Democratic National Convention in Atlantic City, New Jersey. In a nationally televised address to the convention, Hamer described the vicious beatings that she and others had endured—"All of this on account we wanted to register, to become first-class citizens," she explained.

Hamer was elected to Congress that year on a ballot distributed by the MFDP, but the state refused to recognize her victory. The Democratic party resisted the MFDP challenge in 1964 but pledged to prohibit the seating of all-white delegations in the future. When the MFDP returned to the 1968 convention, forcing the Democratic party to make good on its promise, Hamer served as a state delegate.

Recognizing the link between blacks' poverty and their political powerlessness, Hamer helped found community improvement organizations, such as Delta Ministry in 1963 and the Freedom Farms Corporation in 1969. She spoke throughout the country about the work necessary to sustain a truly democratic electoral system and about the sanctity of human rights. Fannie Lou Hamer died of cancer at the age of 60.

FURTHER READING
Mills, Kay. *This Little Light of Mine: The Life of Fannie Lou Hamer.* New York: Dutton, 1993.
Rubel, David. *Fannie Lou Hamer: From Sharecropping to Politics.* Englewood Cliffs, N.J.: Silver Burdett, 1990.

◇ ◇ ◇

Harper, Frances Ellen Watkins

ACTIVIST, WRITER

*Born: September 24, 1825
Baltimore, Maryland*

*Died: February 20, 1911
Philadelphia, Pennsylvania*

Orphaned at the age of three, Frances Ellen Watkins grew up in the custody of her aunt and uncle, Henrietta and William Watkins, Sr. She received her early education at the Academy for Negro Youth, run by her uncle, a minister and well-known radical abolitionist. At age thirteen, Frances took a job with a white family as a dressmaker and children's nurse. Her employer, a bookseller, allowed her to borrow titles from his store, enabling Frances to continue her education on her own. In 1846, at the age of twenty-one, she published her first collection of poems, *Forest Leaves.*

Four years later, when her aunt and uncle joined an exodus of free blacks to Canada, Frances also left Baltimore, teaching first in Ohio and then in Pennsylvania and New England. She soon joined the abolitionist movement, traveling as a lecturer for the Maine and Pennsylvania Anti-Slavery Societies. At a time when it was still uncommon (and for many people, unacceptable) for a woman to travel unescorted or to speak in public, Frances Watkins maintained a grueling schedule which took her from the Atlantic seaboard to Ohio and Michigan, lecturing to both black and white audiences. Watkins preached and practiced a radical abolitionism that included support for the Free Produce Movement (a group that promoted economic boycotts of slave-produced goods) and public support for John and Mary Brown and the raid on Harpers Ferry. In letters to antislavery newspapers, Watkins also argued that free black men and women must be ensured improved economic opportunities.

Throughout the antebellum period Watkins published her poems (including "Bury Me In A Free Land") in newspapers such as William Lloyd Garrison's *Liberator* and *Frederick Douglass' Paper.* In 1854 her second book, *Poems on Miscellaneous Subjects,* which included "The Slave Mother," included an introduction by Garrison. Her 1859 "Two Offers," a story addressing women's independence that appeared in *Anglo-African* magazine, was the first short story published by an African-American woman. During her public appearances Watkins sold her books and contributed substantial portions of the proceeds to aid fugitive slaves.

Following her 1860 marriage to Fenton Harper, a widower with three children, Frances limited her speaking appearances to the vicinity of their farm near Columbus, Ohio. After her husband's death in 1864, she returned east with her daughter, Mary, born in 1862. After the Civil War, she traveled and lectured throughout the South, speaking to both integrated and all-black audiences. She often lectured to audiences made up only of black women, appearances for which she accepted no payment. Harper drew upon these travels to write *Sketches of Southern Life* (1872), a poetic history of Reconstruction, told through the eyes of an ex-slave woman, Aunt Chloe.

Frances Harper was by now a prominent advocate of women's rights, temperance, and black economic development. Partially because of connections made in her years of antislavery work, she was one of the few black women to attain positions of prominence in those national women's organizations that were predominantly white. In her 1866 address to the National Women's Rights Convention in New York, Harper challenged white women to address issues of racial discrimination. Harper also campaigned for woman suffrage and worked tirelessly for the Women's Christian Temperance Union, serving as the Superintendent of Colored Work at the same time as she publicly criticized racist practices within the organization.

In 1892 Frances Ellen Watkins Harper published her most acclaimed work, the novel *Iola Leroy, Or, Shadows Uplifted.* As black women's clubs were organized across the country in the early 1890s, many took on Harper's name, a

testament to her popularity and influence. Harper was a founding member of the National Association of Colored Women and was elected vice-president in 1897. She died in 1911 in Philadelphia, two years after the death of her daughter Mary.

SELECTED PUBLICATIONS
Moses: A Story on the Nile (1869)
Sketches of Southern Life (1872)
Iola Leroy, Or, Shadows Uplifted (1892)
Complete Poems of Frances E. W. Harper (1988)

FURTHER READING
Boyd, Melba Joyce. *Discarded Legacy: Politics and Poetics in the Life of Frances E. W. Harper, 1825–1911.* Detroit: Wayne State University Press, 1994.
Collier-Thomas, Bettye. "Frances Ellen Watkins Harper: Abolitionist and Feminist Reformer, 1825–1911," in Ann Gordon, ed. *African American Women and the Vote, 1837–1965.* Amherst: University of Massachusetts Press, 1997.

◇ ◇ ◇

Hastie, William Henry

LAWYER, JUDGE, EDUCATOR

Born: November 17, 1904
Knoxville, Tennessee

Died: April 14, 1976
Philadelphia, Pennsylvania

Much of the success of the civil rights movement took place in the legal realm. William Henry Hastie, along with his cousin, Charles Hamilton Houston, and Thurgood Marshall, helped to devise the strategies used by the National Association for the Advancement of Colored People (NAACP) to combat segregation. As members of the Howard University Law School faculty, they combined teaching and activism, turning the law school into a leading institution for the study of constitutional law and opening up educational opportunities for all citizens.

Hastie was an excellent student from high school through law school. At Dunbar High School in Washington, D.C., he was the valedictorian of his class in 1921. At Amherst College in Massachusetts, Hastie won prizes in mathematics and physics and was elected to Phi Beta Kappa. He graduated magna cum laude and was again class valedictorian. At Harvard Law School, he was an editor of the *Harvard Law Review*.

Upon his return to Washington, D.C., Hastie opened a law firm with his father and began teaching at Howard University's law school. The NAACP brought its first legal suits against graduate schools that discriminated against blacks. Unsuccessful in their first case, Hastie and the other lawyers learned how to prepare and argue for successive cases.

Effective legal counsel, as well as a fair court system, were key to the improvement of life for African Americans. During Hastie's reign at Howard University, there was only one black lawyer for every 10,000 African Americans, while the ratio of white lawyers to potential white clients was 1 to 700. Hastie and his colleagues were well aware of the great need for Howard University to produce future civil rights lawyers.

In 1937 Hastie accepted an appointment as federal judge of the U.S. District Court for the Virgin Islands. Seven years later he was appointed governor of the Virgin Islands. In between these two appointments he served as dean of Howard's law school. Hastie was appointed to the Third Circuit Court of

Appeals in Philadelphia in 1949 and remained there for the rest of his career.

FURTHER READING

McGuire, Phillip. *He, Too, Spoke for Democracy: Judge Hastie, World War II, and the Black Soldier*. New York: Greenwood, 1988.
Ware, Gilbert. *William Hastie: Grace Under Pressure*. New York: Oxford University Press, 1984.

Hatcher, Richard
POLITICIAN, ACTIVIST

*Born: July 19, 1933
Michigan City, Indiana*

Richard Hatcher was born and raised in Michigan City, Indiana, the son of Carleton and Catherine Hatcher. He earned a bachelor's degree from Indiana University in 1956 and a law degree from Valparaiso University in 1959. He then moved to Gary, Indiana, where he opened a private law firm and worked for the Lake County prosecutor's office. Hatcher joined the many civil rights battles in Gary. He worked to stop discrimination against blacks in hospitals and in the housing market, he investigated cases of alleged police brutality, and he led a local delegation to the 1963 March on Washington.

Elected to Gary's city council that year, Hatcher quickly earned a reputation as an honest, independently minded leader who was committed to passing civil rights legislation. In 1967, Hatcher was the first African American to be elected mayor of Gary. Although he attracted 10 percent of Gary's white voters, most of the city's white establishment read his victory as a signal to abandon the city. Many white-owned business interests quickly relocated to the neighboring community of Merrillville, thus draining Gary of much-needed jobs and tax payments. The decline of the region's heavy industries only further aggravated the city's economic problems. Hatcher was able to finance the city's basic services by raising taxes and issuing municipal bonds. During his 10 years in office, he also integrated the Gary police force and supported the development of local, black-owned businesses.

Hatcher saw his local, national, and even his international political activities as closely linked. During frequent trips to Washington, D.C., he worked to ensure that Gary received a fair share of federal funds. In 1969, Hatcher participated in an investigation of government-sanctioned violence against the Black Panther party. Three years later, Hatcher helped lead the opening session of the first National Black Political Convention, in Gary. Through his efforts on the board of Trans-Africa, Hatcher helped push the U.S. government to impose economic sanctions against South Africa's apartheid government.

Hatcher served as vice chairman of the Democratic National Committee and won a promise from the party to award contracts to minority-owned businesses. He served on the board of Operation PUSH from 1982 to 1984 and helped organize Jesse Jackson's two campaigns for the Presidency. By the time he left office in 1988, Hatcher was one of the most influential blacks in U.S. party politics.

Hatcher failed to win the mayor's office back in 1991. Since 1988, he has operated his own law firm in Gary and has worked to support black-owned businesses in the United States.

FURTHER READING

Cheers, Michael. "Richard Hatcher: Dean of Black Politics," *Ebony*, August 1984.
Haskins, James. *A Piece of the Power: Four Black Mayors.* New York: Dial, 1972.

Henderson, Fletcher

BANDLEADER, COMPOSER, PIANIST

Born: December 18, 1897
Cuthbert, Georgia

Died: December 29, 1952
New York, New York

Fletcher Henderson grew up in a middle-class family. His mother taught piano, an instrument that Henderson began to play at age six. He studied math and chemistry at Atlanta University and moved to New York after graduation in 1920. Unable to find employment as a chemist, he worked as a music demonstrator and eventually as an assistant at Black Swan Records, the first black-owned recording company. Henderson began to assemble back-up bands for Black Swan recordings and by 1924 had formed his own group. That year he took a position as bandleader at the Roseland Ballroom in New York.

Like so many middle-class blacks of the era, Henderson had been exposed mostly to European classical music as a child and young adult. Consequently, black folk music, spirituals, and early jazz had little or no influence on his early arrangements for the dance band. In the 1920s, however, Henderson began to study jazz, and he invited young jazz innovators into his orchestra. The contributions of Louis Armstrong (a soloist in the band from 1924 to 1925) and Don Redman (who arranged Henderson's material until 1927) helped transform the orchestra into the most influential jazz band of its time. After Redman's departure, Henderson did most of the arrangements himself, and his delicate, swinging style became the principal model for big band jazz.

Henderson attracted terrific young talent to the orchestra, helping to launch the careers of many important jazz soloists. In addition to Armstrong and Redman, artists including Coleman Hawkins, Roy Eldridge, Billie Holiday, Benny Carter, Chu Berry, and Lester Young got their starts with Henderson. During his years in the big band, Hawkins helped establish the tenor saxophone as a legitimate solo voice in jazz.

The band's popularity waned by the mid-1930s. Many musicians were driven away by Henderson's poor management of business affairs, and the orchestra's performances began to reflect the disarray. Strapped for cash, Henderson sold several of his arrangements to Benny Goodman, and he eventually joined Goodman's big band as an arranger in 1939. Henderson's influence on the Goodman orchestra—the band which helped make swing music enormously popular with white audiences after 1935—is unmistakable. Henderson continued to arrange for big bands and perform throughout the country, until a stroke paralyzed him in 1950.

FURTHER READING

Stewart, Rex. *Jazz Masters of the Thirties.* New York: Macmillan, 1972.
Williams, Martin. *The Jazz Tradition.* New York: Oxford University Press, 1983.

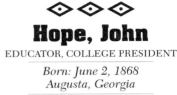

Hope, John

EDUCATOR, COLLEGE PRESIDENT

Born: June 2, 1868
Augusta, Georgia

Died: February 20, 1936
Atlanta, Georgia

John Hope's mother, Mary Frances Butts, was the daughter of a former slave. His father, James Hope, was a white man born in Scotland. John worked part-time from the age of 10, and at 13 he left school to work for a restaurant. He returned to school five years later, eventually graduating from the Worcester Academy in Massachusetts in 1890. At Brown University, Hope edited the school paper, played baseball and football, and joined the debating society. He graduated in 1894.

From 1894 until 1898, Hope taught science, Greek, and Latin in Nashville, Tennessee. He married Lugenia D. Burns, a social worker, in 1897. The following year, Hope moved to Atlanta Baptist College (renamed Morehouse College in 1913). He taught classics, coached the football team, and from 1906 until 1931 served as the college's president.

In addition to raising money for the school, Hope helped attract leading black scholars such as Benjamin Brawley, John Brown Watson, Samuel Howard Archer, and William J. Bauduit to teach there and serve in administrative positions. During the 1920s, Hope and his new colleagues skillfully used donated funds to build the "Greater Morehouse." They dramatically increased enrollment, modernized and expanded campus facilities, and established an important school of social work.

During his early years at Atlanta Baptist, Hope developed a close friendship with W. E. B. Du Bois, who had accepted a position at Atlanta University in 1897. Both men believed that black people should have the right to university educations and not restrict themselves solely to "vocational" training, as Booker T. Washington and others recommended at the time. Hope participated in important early civil rights meetings with Du Bois, including the 1895 Macon Convention, the 1906 meeting of the Niagara Movement, and the protest meeting in New York that led to the creation of the NAACP in 1909. Hope was often the only college president to publicly support these protest efforts.

In 1929 Hope was appointed president of the new Atlanta University consortium—which at that time included Morehouse College, Atlanta University, and Spelman College—where he helped establish important graduate and professional programs. Atlanta University also sponsored annual conferences for black high school educators and a citizenship school that encouraged black Atlantans to vote.

Throughout his life Hope worked with numerous civic and political organizations, including the National Association of Colored Schools, the NAACP, the National Urban League, and the Association for the Study of Negro Life and History. He advised international organizations on issues of world peace, racial conflict, and the status of colonial subjects. Working with the YMCA in France during World War I, Hope witnessed white Americans' mistreatment of black soldiers. Although he was disillusioned about the prospects for improving black–white relations,

he eventually accepted an invitation to join the Commission on Interracial Cooperation, and was appointed its president in 1932.

FURTHER READING
Bacote, Clarence A. *The Story of Atlanta University: A Century of Service, 1865–1965.* Atlanta: Atlanta University, 1969.
Torrence, Ridgely. *The Story of John Hope.* New York: Macmillan, 1948.

Horne, Lena
ACTRESS, SINGER

Born: June 30, 1917
Brooklyn, New York

Horne was raised in a middle-class family of intellectuals, activists, and artists. She attended public schools in Brooklyn, where she spent much of her childhood with her grandparents and other relatives. She also studied in small towns throughout the South while traveling with her mother, an aspiring actress. Lena began performing at age six. At 16 she left school to join the chorus line at Harlem's Cotton Club. The following year she made her first appearance on Broadway.

In 1936, Horne recorded with bandleader Noble Sissle and toured the nation with Sissle's Orchestra. Successful nightclub stints in New York and Hollywood followed. These years marked a turning point for Horne and the beginning of an illustrious career in recording, stage, and film. Horne's film debut came in 1938 in the all-black musical *The Duke Is Tops.* Three years later she signed with MGM, becoming the first black performer to win a long-term contract with a major film studio.

Insisting that she not be cast in stereotypical roles, Horne usually played the part of a talented, self-assured, and glamorous entertainer. She appeared in many popular movies—including *Stormy Weather* (1943)—that introduced audiences to an image of blacks never before seen in Hollywood cinema.

In the 1950s Horne made her first television appearance and had her first starring role on Broadway, in *Jamaica* (1957). Highly in demand on stage, in film, and in recording studios, Horne became one of the most widely recognized entertainers of the era. Her popularity endured, as she recorded, toured, and made countless film and television appearances throughout the 1960s and 1970s. Her one-woman Broadway show, *Lena Horne: The Lady and Her Music* (1981), earned her a Grammy Award for best female pop vocalist.

Throughout her career, Horne has been an outspoken advocate of human and civil rights. While performing on American military bases during World War II, she refused to accept payment from the U.S. Army when she discovered that blacks were segregated in the audience. Horne worked with the Council of African Affairs and several black women's organizations, and she was a vocal defender of the rights of Japanese Americans in California following the war. Because of her political activities and her friendships with prominent activists, Horne was placed on the Hollywood blacklist during the 1950s, which kept her out of film and television for several years. In the 1960s, she was one of many black celebrities to actively support the civil rights movement.

FURTHER READING

Buckley, Gail Lumet. *The Hornes: An American Family.* New York: Knopf, 1986.
Horne, Lena, and Richard Schickel. *Lena.* 1965. Reprint, New York: Harper & Row, 1986.
Palmer, Leslie. *Lena Horne.* New York: Chelsea House, 1989.

◇ ◇ ◇

Houston, Charles Hamilton

LAWYER, EDUCATOR

Born: September 3, 1895
Washington, D.C.

Died: April 22, 1950
Washington, D.C.

Charles Houston was the son of William Houston, an attorney, and Mary Hamilton Houston, who taught school and worked as a hairdresser. After attending segregated schools in the District of Columbia, Houston graduated Phi Beta Kappa from Amherst College in 1915. He was the only black student in his graduating class. He taught English at Howard University and served in the army during World War I, then was a spectacular student in the law schools of Harvard University and the University of Madrid.

Houston passed the District of Columbia bar in 1924 and joined his father's law firm. Charles practiced law there throughout his life, while working with a number of educational and civil rights organizations and publishing columns on a variety of national and international issues. Quickly establishing himself as an important voice in legal education and reform, Houston was appointed vice dean of the law school at Howard University in 1929. Houston led the transformation of the law school from a part-time night school into a full-time program that was accredited. By the mid-1930s, Howard had become a unique center for the education of reform-minded, activist black lawyers.

Houston and his colleagues recognized that Southern state legislatures would not voluntarily dismantle Jim Crow segregation laws or give blacks the right to vote. Building upon an older tradition of legal reform, these lawyers believed that by challenging racist laws in the federal courts, blacks could help shape government policies that were more socially responsible.

Beginning in 1935 Houston began serving as special legal counsel for the NAACP. For more than a decade, Houston helped lead a step-by-step legal assault on segregation, which included ground-breaking cases involving public education, employment practices, and housing (including *University of Maryland* v. *Murray*, 1935, an important challenge to the racial segregation of professional schools). By initiating this calculated legal assault on racist institutions, Houston and his colleagues (including Thurgood Marshall) helped force the federal government to take responsibility for protecting the civil rights of African Americans. The work of Houston, his students, and other Howard-trained lawyers continues to have a dramatic impact on constitutional law and civil rights in the United States.

FURTHER READING

McNeil, Genna Rae. *Groundwork: Charles Hamilton Houston and the Struggle for Civil Rights.* Philadelphia: University of Pennsylvania Press, 1983.
Tushnet, Mark V. *Making Civil Rights Law: Thurgood Marshall and the Supreme Court, 1936–1961.* New York: Oxford University Press, 1994.

◇ ◇ ◇
Hudson, Hosea
COMMUNIST PARTY ACTIVIST,
ORGANIZATIONAL LEADER

Born: April 12, 1898
Wilkes County, Georgia

Died: October 30, 1988
Gainesville, Florida

Hosea Hudson was a Communist party member for over 50 years. Raised in the Deep South where he had to endure racism, segregation, low pay, and class tensions, Hudson was attracted to the Communist party more than organizations like the NAACP. For Hudson, the Communist party provided a vehicle to fight against race and class oppression, to learn to read and write, and to travel. Hudson was part of a small but significant group of black southerners who believed that workers had to unite across racial lines to achieve justice and equality.

Hosea Hudson grew up in a sharecropping family in rural Georgia that struggled financially and moved often to find work. Hudson began plowing at age 10. His next job was at a sawmill where he worked six days a week for 50 cents a day. When Hudson was 15, his mother left him with his brother and grandmother, forcing Hudson to be responsible for the economic livelihood of the family. Pushed from Wilkes County by the boll weevil, family tensions, and lack of work, Hudson moved to Atlanta in 1923. Unsuccessful in his attempts to find work as a machinist, he moved to Birmingham, Alabama, where he found a job as an iron worker.

There were no organizations for working-class blacks in the South before the Communist party began organizing in 1929. Hudson did not feel welcome at the National Association for the Advancement of Colored People meetings, which were run by middle-class blacks. He was recruited into the party by one of his former co-workers, Al Murphy, who saw Hudson as a perfect candidate because of his standing at the foundry and because he was well known throughout the community for his singing in a quartet. Hudson and others risked much by joining the Communist party—condemnation from their community and family as well as loss of their jobs. Hudson had the specific task of overseeing the unemployment councils in Birmingham.

In the 1930s, blacks constituted about 10 percent of the national membership of the Communist party. The Birmingham chapter as well as other chapters in the Deep South were predominantly black; elsewhere in the country membership was predominantly white.

Hudson stayed a member of the party throughout his life. Although he did not learn to read and write until he was 36, Hudson wrote an autobiography, *Black Worker in the Deep South,* in 1972.

FURTHER READING
Painter, Nell. *The Narrative of Hosea Hudson.* Cambridge: Harvard University Press, 1979.

Hughes, James Mercer Langston

WRITER

Born: February 1, 1902
Joplin, Missouri

Died: May 27, 1967
New York, New York

One of this century's most accomplished writers, Langston Hughes devoted his career to depicting and celebrating the lives of African Americans. Hughes was on the move throughout his life. He attended elementary school in Topeka, Kansas, then lived in Lincoln, Illinois, and Cleveland, Ohio. After graduating from high school, he lived with his father in Mexico. He attended Columbia University for a year in 1921, then traveled in Africa and Europe, working at times as a seaman and dishwasher. In 1921, he published one of his most famous poems, "The Negro Speaks of Rivers," in *The Crisis* magazine. Upon returning to the United States he worked as a researcher for Carter Woodson at the Association for the Study of Negro Life and History, and published his first volume of poetry, *The Weary Blues* (1926).

After graduating from Lincoln University in Pennsylvania in 1929, Hughes set out to make a living as a writer. Aided by a white patron, he published his first novel, *Not Without Laughter,* in 1930. With encouragement from Mary McLeod Bethune, he traveled throughout the southern and western United States, reading his poems at numerous black colleges. He visited Cuba, Haiti, the Soviet Union, and Japan. After returning to the U.S. in 1933, Hughes lived in Carmel, California, supporting his mother and brother by writing and reading poetry, and later moved to Oberlin, Ohio. During the 1930s, several of Hughes's plays were produced in Cleveland and New York City. He served as a war correspondent in Madrid in 1937, and established the Harlem Suitcase Theater in New York in 1938. Much of his work from this period reflected his interest in radical politics.

In 1942, Hughes began a weekly column in the Chicago *Defender*. The following year, he introduced to the column a character named Jesse B. Semple (or "Simple"), a politically savvy and very funny black workingman. Hughes's "conversations" with Simple—about subjects including neighborhood news, personal relationships, black history, and racism— were later collected in five volumes, the first appearing in 1950 (*Simple Speaks His Mind*). In 1952 Hughes published one of his most famous collections of stories, *Laughing to Keep From Crying*. His highly regarded volumes of poetry include *One-Way Ticket* (1949) and *Montage of a Dream Deferred* (1951). In all these works, Hughes developed distinctive new styles of writing and storytelling that were deeply influenced by black speech, by jazz, and by the blues.

Hughes also wrote for film, musicals, and operas and translated fiction and poetry from French and Spanish. He edited several volumes of black poetry and humor and collaborated on pictorial histories of African Americans, including *The Sweet Flypaper of Life* (1955) and *Black Magic: A Pictorial History of the Negro in American Entertainment* (1967). His numerous children's books include *Famous American Negroes*, *The First Book of Jazz*, *The First Book of the Caribbean*, and *Black Misery*. Hughes described his travels, his experiences, and the numerous influences on his literary work in two volumes of autobiography, *The Big Sea* (1940) and *I Wonder as I Wander* (1956). He settled in Harlem in 1947 and lived there until his death at the age of 65.

SELECTED PUBLICATIONS
The Weary Blues (1926)
Not Without Laughter (1930)
The Big Sea (1940)
I Wonder as I Wander (1956)
The Best of Simple (1961)
The Collected Poems of Langston Hughes (1994)

FURTHER READING
Rampersad, Arnold. *The Life of Langston Hughes*. 2 vols. New York: Oxford University Press, 1986, 1988.
Rummel, Jack. *Langston Hughes.* New York: Chelsea House, 1988.

Hurston, Zora Neale
ANTHROPOLOGIST, FOLKLORIST, WRITER

Born: January 7, 1891
Eatonville, Florida

Died: January 28, 1960
Fort Pierce, Florida

From the Harlem Renaissance through the 1940s, Zora Neale Hurston wrote about the joy and beauty of black folks. As an anthropologist, Hurston traveled throughout the South observing and collecting folklore—stories, jokes, dances, and songs. For Hurston, these expressions came from complex, creative beings, not victims ravaged by racism and poverty, as she felt many of her colleagues portrayed blacks.

Hurston was raised in Eatonville, Florida, the first incorporated black township in the country. Her father, Reverend John Hurston, served three terms as mayor and her mother, Lucy Ann Hurston, taught Sunday school. Hurston was therefore accustomed to seeing blacks fulfilling the whole range of roles and responsibilities required to run a town.

After her mother's death in 1904, Hurston left Eatonville and worked as a maid and wardrobe assistant with a traveling show. When the troupe arrived in Baltimore, Maryland, Hurston decided to enter Morgan Academy, a high school. After graduation in 1918, she attended Howard University in Washington, D.C.

She pursued her writing while an undergraduate; her first story was published in the university's literary magazine, *Stylus*, in 1921. Four years later, she left for New York. Hurston quickly became part of the black literary world. In 1926 she collaborated with writers and artists Gwendolyn Bennett, Richard Bruce, John Davis, Aaron Douglass, Langston Hughes, and Wallace Thurman on *Fire!!: A Quarterly Devoted to the Younger Negro Artists*. Unfortunately, because of lack of money and a fire that destroyed a few hundred copies of the issue, only one issue was published. Her play *Color Struck* and a short story, *Sweat*, appeared in this issue.

Hurston received a scholarship to Barnard College in New York City, where she studied anthropology under Franz Boas. She continued to study with him on the graduate level at Columbia University. Boas encouraged Hurston to return to her hometown and collect folklore, which she did with financial support from Mrs. Osgood Mason, a white socialite. Hurston is credited with being the first African American to collect and publish black folklore from the United States and the Caribbean.

Hurston published four novels, an autobiography, two books of folklore, and numerous articles and stories. She was able to support herself through her writing. By the early 1950s, however, she resorted to odd jobs for subsistence. In 1959 she suffered a stroke and checked into a welfare home, where she died penniless a few months later.

PUBLICATIONS
Mules and Men (1935)
Their Eyes Were Watching God (1937)
Tell My Horse (1938)
Dust Tracks on a Road: An Autobiography (1942)

FURTHER READING
Hemenway, Robert E. *Zora Neale Hurston: A Literary Biography*. Urbana: University of Illinois Press, 1977.
Lyons, Mary E. *Sorrow's Kitchen: The Life and Folklore of Zora Neale Hurston.* New York: Scribners, 1990.

Jackson, Jesse
ACTIVIST, MINISTER, POLITICIAN

Born: October 8, 1941
Greenville, South Carolina

When Jesse Jackson attended Sterling High School in Greenville, South Carolina, he worked part time to help support his family and devoted time to the local Baptist church. As the star quarterback on Sterling's football team, he led the squad to the state football championship. Jackson rejected an athletic scholarship from the University of Illinois when he discovered that the football team would not allow blacks to play anything but linemen positions. Instead, he accepted a football scholarship at North Carolina State College in Greensboro, a black school, where he started as quarterback and studied sociology and economics.

In 1963 Jackson was elected student body president, and he helped organize pickets and sit-ins to battle segregation in restaurants and theaters. Upon graduation in 1964, he worked for the governor of North Carolina until he left to study at the Chicago Theological Seminary and to work part time for the Southern Christian Leadership Conference (SCLC).

Jackson left the seminary in 1966 to run the Chicago branch of Operation Breadbasket, an SCLC organization that led boycotts and pickets against businesses that discriminated against African Americans. In 1967 Martin Luther King, Jr., appointed him Operation Breadbasket's national director. Jackson grew disenchanted with the SCLC after King's death and founded Operation PUSH (People United to Save Humanity) in 1971. By the mid-1970s, PUSH was a well-funded national organization and Jackson was touring the country, encouraging school-aged children and young adults to stay in school and to avoid drug use and teenage pregnancy.

Beginning in 1979, Jackson traveled extensively around the world. He visited South Africa and condemned the white government's system of racial apartheid. He visited the Middle East and urged the Israeli government to negotiate with the Palestine Liberation Organization. While many Americans applauded Jackson's initiatives, others condemned him for associating with international figures who they considered to be enemies of the United States.

In 1984, Jackson ran for President of the United States on a platform focusing on the rights of the poor and dispossessed. He hoped to garner the support of what he called a "Rainbow Coalition" of minorities, white liberals, and all those voters who felt estranged by the leadership and policies of the Reagan administration. Jackson won 21 percent of the popular vote in the primary elections. But his campaign was constrained by a limited budget and by the fact that many prominent black politicians and civil rights activists refused to endorse his candidacy.

Jackson continued to speak internationally in the late 1980s. By running for President again in 1988, Jackson forced the Democrats to recognize the voting power of the Rainbow Coalition and thus to adopt a more progressive party platform. In 1990, the voters of Washington, D.C., elected him their "shadow" senator, a position intended to draw attention to the political disenfranchisement of the city.

PUBLICATION
Straight from the Heart (1987)

FURTHER READING
Collins, Sheila D. *The Rainbow Challenge: The Jackson Campaign and the Future of U.S. Politics*. New York: Monthly Review Press, 1986.
Haskins, James. *I Am Somebody!: A Biography of Jesse Jackson*. Hillside, N.J.: Enslow, 1992.
Jakoubek, Robert E. *Jesse Jackson*. New York: Chelsea House, 1991.
Reynolds, Barbara A. *Jesse Jackson: The Man, The Movement, The Myth*. Chicago: Nelson-Hall, 1975.

◇ ◇ ◇
Jackson, Mahalia
GOSPEL SINGER

Born: October 26, 1911
New Orleans, Louisiana

Died: January 27, 1972
Evergreen Park, Illinois

Mahalia Jackson grew up in a poor, working-class neighborhood near the riverfront in New Orleans. Her father moved cotton on the New Orleans docks during the day, worked as a barber at night, and preached in the local church on Sundays. Her mother died when Mahalia was just five years old, so Mahalia and her brother moved in with their aunt, Mahalia Paul. Jackson began singing at a very early age, and especially enjoyed singing with the congregation at her father's church, the Mount Moriah Baptist Church. Mahalia grew up in a deeply devout Baptist family, and the church would remain central both to her life and her music. "My strength," she explained at the peak of her fame in the 1960s, "has always been in the church and I'll never leave it."

Jackson's singing was influenced by other traditions as well. The music that she heard from a Sanctified church next door to her family's home shaped her approach to gospel. And in the black neighborhoods of New Orleans, she was surrounded by ragtime and the blues, by the early jazz being performed in local clubs, by riverboat bands, and by the brass bands that advertised fish fries and house-rent parties. She listened avidly to the phonograph recordings of blues artists that were so popular in these years (her favorite blues singers were Bessie Smith and Ma Rainey). Although she never made blues recordings, the blues tradition had an important influence on Jackson's distinctive approach to gospel singing.

In 1927 she moved to Chicago to live with her aunt, Hannah, and to pursue a musical career. Jackson worked as a hotel maid, eventually saving up enough money to open a beauty shop. But her focus was on singing, and she quickly established her reputation as one of the most dynamic voices in gospel, primarily through her

seven-year stint with the Johnson Singers. By 1941 she was singing as a soloist. While she began recording gospel music in 1934, it was her switch to the Apollo label and her recording of "Move On Up a Little Higher" (1947) that brought her to the attention of a national audience. "Move On Up" sold millions of copies, making it one of the first gold records in gospel.

Soon thereafter, Jackson was chosen as the official soloist for the National Baptist Convention and began to tour the United States. In 1954 she became the first gospel singer to host a national radio show. Her fame continued to grow as she appeared on national television programs, at music festivals, and in movies, and as she began to tour internationally. At the request of civil rights leaders, Jackson sang at a demonstration in support of the Birmingham bus boycott, and she continued to support black political causes throughout her life. In 1963, in one of her most celebrated performances, Jackson sang for the participants in the March on Washington.

PUBLICATION
Movin' On Up (1966)

FURTHER READING
Gourse, Leslie. *Mahalia Jackson: Queen of Gospel Song*. New York: Watts, 1996.
Schwerin, Jules Victor. *Got to Tell It: Mahalia Jackson, Queen of Gospel*. New York: Oxford University Press, 1992.

◇ ◇ ◇

Jackson, Maynard Holbrook, Jr.

LAWYER, POLITICIAN
Born: March 23, 1938
Dallas, Texas

Maynard Jackson's father, Maynard, Sr., was a Baptist minister and the first black person to run for a seat on the Texas board of education. Jackson's mother, Irene Dobbs Jackson, would later chair the foreign language department at North Carolina Central University. When Maynard, Jr., was seven years old, the family moved to Atlanta. Jackson excelled in the city's segregated schools and at the age of 14 was admitted to Morehouse College as a Ford Foundation Early Admissions Scholar. After graduating in 1956, he worked in Cleveland for the state of Ohio, and then in Buffalo, Boston, and Cleveland as a salesman and district sales manager for the P. F. Collier Company, an encyclopedia publisher. He then returned to school, earning a law degree from North Carolina Central in 1964.

Jackson returned to Atlanta, where he handled unfair labor practice cases for the federal National Labor Relations Board. He later provided legal assistance to poor Atlanta residents as counsel for the Emory Community Legal Service Center. Through his work on behalf of working people and minorities, and a failed election bid for the U.S. Senate in 1968, Jackson received a great deal of political exposure and earned a wide following among blacks and liberal whites in Atlanta. In 1969 he became Atlanta's first black vice mayor. While in office, Jackson supported grassroots political networks and neighborhood coalitions, expanding his support among the city's electorate. In 1973, at the age of 34, he overcame a racially charged campaign to be elected the city's first black mayor.

Jackson served two consecutive terms, from 1974 to 1982, and was reelected for a third term in 1989. He created a city program to support minority-owned businesses, and increased the number of minorities and white women who received government jobs and municipal contracts. Because Atlanta's minority-owned firms were receiving only 1 percent of the city's construction contracts, Jackson delayed work on the city's international airport until minority-owned firms received a larger percentage. While Jackson angered many white business people and political leaders with such tactics, he increased the amount of city and federal money that went to minority-owned businesses and minority employees in Atlanta.

In part because of Jackson's leadership, several sectors of Atlanta's economy flourished during the 1980s and early 1990s, and more African Americans were able to attain positions of political and economic power. At the same time, Jackson was often criticized for paying more attention to the interests of business people than to the interests of the underprivileged. After leaving office in 1993, Jackson returned to work as chairman of an investment banking firm that he had founded in 1987.

FURTHER READING
Slaughter, John. *New Battles Over Dixie: The Campaign for a New South.* Dix Hills, N.Y.: General Hall, 1992.

Johnson, Charles Spurgeon

SCHOLAR, EDITOR

Born: July 24, 1893
Bristol, Virginia

Died: October 27, 1956
Louisville, Kentucky

Through his influential scholarship and work as an adviser, Charles Johnson helped draw the attention of government officials, academics, and activists to the economic foundations of racial inequality. He was the son of Winifred Branch Johnson and the Reverend Charles Henry Johnson, a Baptist minister. Johnson started college early and graduated from Virginia Union University in 1916. While working on a graduate degree in sociology at the University of Chicago, Johnson served as Director of Research and Records for the Chicago Urban League.

After the Chicago race riot in 1919, Johnson was appointed to the Chicago Commission on Race Relations, which investigated the origins of the violence. Johnson coauthored the commission's report, *The Negro in Chicago: A Study in Race Relations and a Race Riot* (1922), which was an important early examination of segregation and white violence against black people in Northern cities. In 1921 he became the director of research for the National Urban League in New York City. Two years later, he was appointed editor of the League's new magazine, *Opportunity,* one of the publications that helped popularize many of the black essayists and poets of the Harlem Renaissance.

From 1927 to 1947 Johnson chaired the department of social sciences at Fisk University, then became president of Fisk in 1947. Johnson helped assemble one of the premier social science faculties in the nation. He helped attract scholars who were committed to enlisting social science in the battle against segregation and discrimination. During his years at Fisk, Johnson published dozens of important articles and books, in which he often focused on how economics and government policy shaped the lives of African Americans and influenced race relations. In *Shadow of the Plantation* (1934), for example, Johnson demonstrated how federal policy accelerated the collapse of black farming in the American South during the Great Depression, thus further endangering the livelihood and the safety of Southern blacks.

Johnson was a consultant to numerous Presidential administrations and a participant in several groups that organized against racism. He joined several international delegations as well, including an investigation of human rights violations in Liberia in 1930. Many reformers saw Johnson as socially conservative. Yet others accused him of being a subversive, even a supporter of communism, because he attacked racial segregation and because he participated in organizations that received support from the radical left.

SELECTED PUBLICATIONS
The Negro in Chicago: A Study in Race Relations and a Race Riot (1922)
The Negro in American Civilization: A Study of Negro Life and Race Relations in the Light of Social Research (1930)
Shadow of the Plantation (1934)

FURTHER READING
Egerton, John. *Speak Now Against the Day: The Generation Before the Civil Rights Movement in the South.* New York: Knopf, 1994.

◇ ◇ ◇
Johnson, James Weldon
WRITER, ACTIVIST, SONGWRITER,
GOVERNMENT OFFICIAL

*Born: July 17, 1871
Jacksonville, Florida*

*Died: June 26, 1938
Wiscasset, Maine*

James Weldon Johnson was raised in Jacksonville, Florida. His mother, Helen Dillet Johnson, originally from the

Bahamas, was a public school teacher. His father, James, Sr., who had been born free in Richmond, Virginia, worked as a waiter and made very successful investments in real estate. Both James, Jr., and his brother Rosamond were avid readers as children, and both played the piano.

James graduated from the Stanton elementary school in 1887. He later attended Atlanta University, where he was particularly successful as a writer and public speaker. Upon graduation in 1894, he returned to Jacksonville to serve as principal of the Stanton school and helped oversee its transformation into Florida's first public high school for blacks. In 1901, Johnson was selected to serve as president of the Florida State Teachers Association. He also studied law and passed the Florida bar.

Johnson was also pursuing his artistic interests, writing lyrics for music composed by his brother Rosamond. In 1900 the two collaborated on "Lift Ev'ry Voice and Sing," a song later dubbed the "Negro National Anthem." In 1902 he moved to New York, where he, his brother, and a friend worked the vaudeville circuit and became successful songwriters. While studying literature at Columbia University, Johnson began to involve himself in New York City politics and the local black Republican organization. As a result of his political work, he was appointed in 1906 to serve as U.S. consul at Puerto Cabello, Venezuela, then at Corinto, Nicaragua, from 1909 to 1913.

Johnson left the foreign service to write editorials for the *New York Age,* a black weekly in New York City. During his tenure there, Johnson contributed hundreds of articles on a wide range of topics, including literature, party politics, race, religion, economics, mob violence, women's rights, poetry, and music. His uncompromising critique of race relations and his advocacy of protest made him an important voice in black politics. And his reviews of black artists helped popularize the movement known as the "Harlem Renaissance."

In 1916 Johnson joined the NAACP as its field secretary. Traveling throughout the United States, he helped expand local branch operations and helped increase the organization's membership tenfold. When he accepted the appointment as Secretary of the NAACP's national office, Johnson became the first black person to hold this post. Along with the assistant secretary, Walter White (who would later succeed Johnson), Johnson provided critical behind-the-scenes support for the NAACP's important legal challenges against segregation and black disenfranchisement. During Johnson's tenure, the NAACP developed into a predominantly black-run and highly influential national civil rights organization.

Johnson resigned his NAACP post in 1930 to teach creative writing and literature at Fisk University. He first wrote poetry while in college, and published his first collection of poems in 1917. Johnson considered black art, poetry, and literature to be inseparable from black politics and argued that African Americans possessed a unique and distinctive artistic voice. Throughout the 1920s, he joined NAACP members, including W. E. B. Du Bois and Jessie Fauset, in publicizing the work of black essayists and poets in *The Crisis.* Johnson edited an anthology of African-American poetry (1922) and, with his brother, a two-volume collection of black spirituals (1925 and 1926).

In 1930 Johnson published *Black Manhattan,* a cultural history of black Harlem. Five years after publishing his autobiography, *Along This Way* (1933), he was killed in an automobile accident.

SELECTED PUBLICATIONS
The Autobiography of an Ex-Coloured Man (1912)
The Book of American Negro Spirituals (1925)
Black Manhattan (1930)
Along This Way (1933, reprint 1973)

FURTHER READING
Levy, Eugene. *James Weldon Johnson: Black Leader, Black Voice.* Chicago: University of Chicago Press, 1973.
Tolbert-Rouchaleau, Jane. *James Weldon Johnson.* New York: Chelsea House, 1988.

Jones, Absalom
POLITICAL AND RELIGIOUS LEADER

Born: 1746
Sussex County, Delaware

Died: February 13, 1818
Philadelphia, Pennsylvania

Jones was born enslaved on a Delaware plantation. In 1762, his owner brought him to Philadelphia, where Jones worked in his master's store and attended classes at a night school for African Americans. In 1770 he married a woman who was also enslaved. Over the next 14 years, Jones, his family, and his friends put aside enough money to purchase both his wife's freedom and his own.

Jones quickly established himself as a leader of Philadelphia's large and growing community of free African Americans. He met Richard Allen in 1786, and the two served as lay preachers to the black members of the St. George's Methodist Episcopal Church. When white church officials attempted to segregate the seating of the congregation by race, Jones, Allen, and the other African-American members of the church marched out of St. George's. They organized the Free African Society, which served as both a non-denominational religious organization and a mutual aid society for its members.

In 1791, Jones and Allen began to lead regular Sunday services. Then, with the assistance of Benjamin Rush and members of Philadelphia's Quaker community, they organized The African Church in July of that year. It was the first independent black church in North America. When Allen and others left The African Church to form the all-black Methodist Bethel Church, Jones remained the sole leader of the congregation. It would be renamed the St. Thomas African Episcopal Church, and Jones would become the first African American to be ordained as a priest in 1804.

Jones saw the black church not solely as a place of worship but also as an institution that could support the education of black people, community self-help projects, and political protest. The St. Thomas church sponsored schools and several benevolent societies for its members. Jones and Allen organized brigades of African Americans to assist the sick and dying during a yellow fever epidemic in 1793. Jones denounced slavery and white racism from the pulpit and in a book that he co-authored with Allen in 1793. And Jones helped lead a group of free black Philadelphians who sent antislavery petitions to the Pennsylvania legislature and to the U.S. Congress in 1799 and 1800. With Allen and

James Forten, a Philadelphia manufacturer, Jones organized an important mass meeting at Bethel Church in 1817, to protest against the colonization movement.

Like Allen, Rush, Forten, and other prominent community and religious leaders of the post-Revolutionary era, Jones worked to forge and sustain institutions that helped support and shape the earliest communities of free urban blacks.

FURTHER READING
Nash, Gary B. "'To Arise Out of the Dust': Absalom Jones and the African Church of Philadelphia, 1785–95." In Nash, ed., *Race, Class and Politics: Essays on American Colonial and Revolutionary Society.* Urbana: University of Illinois Press, 1986.
Smith, Edward D. *Climbing Jacob's Ladder: The Rise of Black Churches in Eastern American Cities, 1740–1877.* Washington, D.C.: Smithsonian Institution, 1988.

◇ ◇ ◇
Jones, M. Sissieretta

OPERA AND THEATER SINGER

Born: January 5, 1869
Portsmouth, Virginia

Died: June 24, 1933
Providence, Rhode Island

Jones was born Matilda Sissieretta Joyner in 1869 (she took the name Jones when she married). Her father, Jerimiah Malachi Joyner, was a former slave who served as pastor of an African-American Methodist church in Portsmouth. He also directed the church choir with Sissieretta's mother, Henrietta, who was an accomplished soprano. Sissieretta sang from her earliest days—at home, at school functions, and at church events.

Soon after the family moved to Providence, Rhode Island, in the mid-1880s, Sissieretta began her formal musical training at the Providence Academy of Music. At the age of 18, she entered the New England Conservatory of Music in Boston to study voice. By the time she made her first professional appearances in 1887 and 1888, Jones had established herself as one of the most talented and promising sopranos of her generation. Later in 1888, she began a six-month tour of the West Indies with the Tennessee Jubilee Singers. During the tour, a New York magazine gave her the nickname "Black Patti," a reference to a famous Italian opera singer, Adelina Patti. (Jones considered the nickname to be both pretentious and degrading, but her managers convinced her to keep it.) In 1892, she was the main attraction at the Grand Negro Jubilee, a performance by black entertainers in New York City attended by 75,000 people.

In the early 1890s, Jones gained international prominence for her solo concerts in the United States, Canada, the West Indies, and Europe. These included appearances at major European opera houses, performances for foreign dignitaries and U.S. Presidents, and a celebrated concert at the Chicago World's Fair in 1893. Jones also toured with a company of black musicians that performed a mixture of popular and concert music.

Despite the acclaim that Jones received for her extraordinary talents, the established opera world, which was controlled by whites, would not hire her for major productions because she was black. In part as a response to this, Jones ended her solo career in 1896 to become the leading soprano for a newly organized company, Black Patti's Troubadours. Only by joining a traveling "colored" show, one that included vaudeville and black minstrel acts, could Jones find a venue in which to perform operatic scenes. The Troubadours were enormously successful, touring the United States until 1916. That year, her professional singing career ended. No commercial recordings were ever made of Sissieretta Jones's performances.

Jones returned to Providence, where she worked for the local church and cared for her mother and two homeless boys. She died a pauper in 1933.

FURTHER READING
Story, Rosalyn M. *And So I Sing: African-American Divas of Opera and Concert.* New York: Warner, 1990.

Kelly, Sharon Pratt

LAWYER, POLITICIAN

Born: January 30, 1944
Washington, D.C.

Sharon Pratt Kelly became the first black woman mayor of a major city when she won the mayoral election in Washington, D.C., in 1990. This was a significant victory considering that in 1991, women served as mayors in only 15 percent of U.S. cities with populations over 10,000.

Kelly graduated from Howard University's undergraduate and law schools in 1965 and 1968, respectively. Beginning in 1971, she worked at her father's general practice law firm. From 1972 to 1976, she served on the faculty of the Antioch School of Law. She began her career with the Potomac Electric Power Company as a lawyer doing contract work in 1976, rising to the position of vice president of public policy in 1990.

Although Kelly had never held an elective public office before 1990, she was very active in party politics from the early 1980s. In 1982, she ran the mayoral campaign for Patricia Robert Harris, former dean of Howard University's law school and former U.S. Secretary of Health and Human Services. She was also the first woman to serve as national treasurer of the Democratic party.

In 1990, Kelly ran for mayor of Washington, D.C., challenging incumbent mayor Marion S. Barry. Kelly's bid for mayor was a long shot, but she did have a few things in her favor. First, she received an early endorsement from the *Washington Post,* the most widely read newspaper in the city. Second, Barry was on trial for possession of drugs, which weakened his reelection bid. Kelly's promise to "clean house with a shovel, not a broom" registered with voters who felt that politics in the district needed a change.

Kelly served just one term as mayor. The city she served was deep in debt and struggling with Congress over federal funding for city programs. Her accomplishments during her term include AIDS initiatives, the automation of city offices, and a successful childhood immunization program.

FURTHER READING
Perl, Peter. "The Mayor's Mystique: The Struggles of Sharon Pratt Kelly." *Washington Post Magazine,* January 31, 1993.

King, Martin Luther, Jr.

MINISTER, CIVIL RIGHTS LEADER

Born: January 15, 1929
Atlanta, Georgia

Died: April 4, 1968
Memphis, Tennessee

The Reverend Dr. Martin Luther King, Jr., is the symbolic embodiment of the modern civil rights movement. A charismatic leader who galvanized and inspired millions toward nonviolent action, King was a co-founder, with Ralph Abernathy, of the Southern Christian Leadership Conference (SCLC) in 1957. Beginning with the successful Montgomery, Alabama, bus boycott in 1955 and 1956, King was catapulted to the front lines of Southern civil rights struggles, taking on the heavy burden of appeasing a number of constituencies—his own conscience, his colleagues, the masses, as well as local and federal officials.

The son and grandson of pastors, King was destined to continue the family tradition. He entered Morehouse College in Atlanta at 15 and while there decided to become a minister. After his graduation in 1948, he attended Crozer Theological Seminary in Pennsylvania. He continued north to study for a Ph.D. in systematic theology at Boston University, graduating in 1955.

King returned to the South to serve as pastor of Dexter Avenue Baptist Church in Montgomery, Alabama. Buoyed by the grassroots organizing of the Women's Political Council (WPC), which was largely responsible for the Montgomery bus boycott, King was elected president of the Montgomery Improvement Association. This was one of the first successful integration efforts in the South.

In 1959 King spent a month in India to study Mahatma Gandhi's philosophy of nonviolence. Upon his return to the United States, he and his family moved to Atlanta. In Atlanta and other cities in the South, King helped organize and inspire college students to conduct sit-ins at segregated restaurants, lunch counters, swimming pools, and libraries. King's participation in demonstrations in Birmingham, Alabama, in 1963, during which television viewers witnessed police abuse of nonviolent adults and children, further pushed him to national and international prominence.

On August 28, 1963, at the March on Washington, King gave his oft-quoted "I Have a Dream" speech, in which he called for integration and racial tolerance. He shared the podium with, among others, John Lewis, one of the founders of the Student Nonviolent Coordinating Committee, whose speech was less uplifting and more critical of the federal government. Becoming ever more popular, King received the Nobel Peace Prize in 1964. In 1966 King went to Chicago, planning to use the same strategies there that had worked in the South. He discovered that Northern and Western urban politics were very different from those he had found in the South. His efforts were largely unsuccessful. When King returned to the South, he also faced opposition from more militant blacks who advocated black separatism as opposed to integration.

In 1967 King broadened his notion of civil rights and spoke out against U.S. aggression in Vietnam. That same year, King and SCLC formed the Poor People's Campaign to address poverty in the United States. King gave his last speech in Memphis, Tennessee, where he led a march of striking sanitation workers. The next day he was assassinated.

PUBLICATIONS

Stride Toward Freedom (1958)
Strength to Love (1963)
Why We Can't Wait (1964)
Where Do We Go From Here: Chaos or Community? (1967)
The Measure of a Man (1968)

FURTHER READING

Branch, Taylor. *Parting the Waters: America in the King Years, 1954–1963.* New York: Simon & Schuster, 1988.
Garrow, David J. *Bearing the Cross: Martin Luther King, Jr., and the Southern Christian Leadership Conference.* New York: William Morrow, 1986.
Jakoubek, Robert. *Martin Luther King, Jr.* New York: Chelsea House, 1989.

Locke, Alain

PHILOSOPHER, WRITER, EDUCATOR

Born: September 13, 1885
Philadelphia, Pennsylvania

Died: June 9, 1954
Washington, D.C.

Locke was born in Philadelphia, a city with a rich history of African-American activism and institution building. As a youngster, despite his battle with rheumatic fever, he played the piano and violin. His parents doted on him, placing him in alternative schools. Locke developed into a brilliant scholar. An honors graduate of Harvard College, selected to Phi Beta Kappa and awarded a Rhodes scholarship to Oxford University in England, Locke devoted his intellectual energy and rigor to matters of race, cultural pluralism, and art.

Locke began teaching in the philosophy department at Howard University in 1912. Locke, along with numerous other scholars, mathematician William J. Baudit, English professor Benjamin Brawley, and biologist Thomas W. Turner, helped to build Howard into a leading research university. Locke's tenure at the university was sometimes rocky. A proposal he submitted in 1915 for a course on "interracial relations" was rejected by the administration, who felt that kind of course inappropriate at that time in history. Ten years later Locke was dismissed for supporting student protesters. Locke returned to Howard three years later.

While Locke spent most of his time with artists, writers, and other scholars, he was also concerned with having materials available to the masses, which led to his participation in the adult education movement. In addition to serving as president of the American Association of Adult Education in 1939, Locke helped to found the Associates in Negro Folk Education, whose purpose was to publish materials on black life that could be used in adult education programs. Locke got leading intellectuals—Ralph Bunche, Abram Harris, Sterling Brown, Carter G. Woodson, and Eugene Kinckle Jones—to write what came to be called "Bronze Booklets."

Locke was a major force in the Negro Renaissance. Editor of the groundbreaking anthology *The New Negro: An Interpretation* (1925), Locke helped define a black aesthetic in the 1920s and 1930s. He served as a mentor to numerous artists and writers, including William H. Johnson and Zora Neale Hurston.

A vigorous promoter of the visual arts and theater, Locke wrote a number of essays exploring the relationship between culture and democracy in the United States and abroad.

Locke's last project was *The Negro in American Culture*, which he was unable to complete before his death.

PUBLICATIONS

The New Negro: An Interpretation (1925, reprint 1992)
The Negro and His Music (1936)
The Negro in Art: A Pictorial Record of the Negro Artists and the Negro Theme in Art (1940)

FURTHER READING

Stewart, Jeffrey C. *A Biography of Alain Locke: Philosopher of the Harlem Renaissance, 1886–1930*. Ann Arbor, Mich.: University Microfilms International, 1981.
Stewart, Jeffrey C., ed. *The Critical Temper of Alain Locke: A Selection of His Essays on Art and Culture*. New York: Garland, 1983.

◇ ◇ ◇
Louis, Joe

BOXER

Born: May 13, 1914
Chambers County, Alabama

Died: April 12, 1981
Las Vegas, Nevada

Joe Louis, the "Brown Bomber," had a tremendous boxing career. Sports have historically been one of the few arenas for black men to gain recognition and financial success. For African Americans, who were offered few opportunities to compete with whites, Joe Louis's victories over white opponents were claimed as victories for "the race." Louis was also a U.S. hero, because of his defeat of international opponents. During the height of Nazism, sports became a political arena in which every victory by Louis was seen as a defeat of Hitler's Germany.

Louis was born into a sharecropping family in rural Alabama. His family moved to Detroit in 1926 so his stepfather could work at the Ford Motor Company. They were part of a continual wave of families seeking better education, recreation, and employment in the North. Louis, who went to school irregularly while in the South, was not advanced enough to attend classes with his age group. He eventually dropped out of school and found work to supplement the family income.

Louis lost the first fight of his amateur career, which began in 1932. Two years later he won the light heavyweight championship of the Amateur Athletic Union. That same year he began competing on the highest level—in the heavyweight division. Louis followed in the footsteps of other black boxers, most notably William Richmond, who in 1805 became the first African American to contend for a world title in any sport, and John Arthur "Jack" Johnson, who was the first black boxer to beat a white world heavyweight champion.

In Louis's first professional match, he knocked out Jack Cracken in the first round. Louis's most famous bouts were against Germany's Max Schmeling. Each boxer became a symbolic figure for his respective country in the years before World War II. In their first fight, on June 19, 1936, Louis was knocked out in the 12th round. This was his first loss as a professional. In their second match, on June 22, 1938, Louis knocked Schmeling out in two minutes. Louis went on to hold the heavyweight title for 11 years. In 1954 he was elected to the Boxing Hall of Fame.

PUBLICATION
My Life Story (1947)

FURTHER READING
Jakoubek, Robert. *Joe Louis.* New York: Chelsea House, 1990.
Mead, Chris. *Champion: Joe Louis, Black Hero in White America*. New York: Scribners, 1985.

Lynch, John Roy

POLITICIAN, LAWYER

Born: September 10, 1847
near Vidalia, Concordia Parish, Louisiana

Died: November 2, 1939
Chicago, Illinois

John Lynch was born enslaved on a plantation in Louisiana. He was one of three children born to Patrick Lynch, a native of Ireland, and Catherine White, an enslaved African-American woman. Shortly before he died, Patrick attempted to free his family, but Catherine and the children were sold to another planter in Natchez, Mississippi. They were eventually freed when the Union army occupied the city in 1863.

After the Civil War, Lynch managed a successful photographic business in Natchez and attended night classes in 1866. When the school abruptly closed, he taught himself how to read and write. Soon after the Reconstruction Act of 1867 opened up new political opportunities for African Americans in the South, Lynch joined the city's Republican club.

In 1869, Lynch was elected to the lower house of the Mississippi legislature. He distinguished himself quickly and took on considerable responsibility within the party. He served on numerous committees and played a major role in sponsoring Republican legislation. In 1872 he was elected speaker of the house.

The following year, at the age of 26, Lynch was elected to the U.S. Congress. Reelected in 1874, he was a prominent supporter of the Civil Rights Bill of 1875. By the time he retired from Congress in 1883, he had become an influential member of the national Republican party.

After leaving Congress, Lynch managed his plantation in Mississippi and bought more real estate in Adams County. He studied law independently in the 1890s, passed the Mississippi bar in 1896, and then joined a Washington law firm. He worked for the U.S. Treasury from 1889 to 1893 and then served in the army, including tours in Cuba and the Philippines, until 1911. Lynch then moved to Chicago, where he practiced law and entered the real estate market.

In 1913, Lynch wrote *The Facts of Reconstruction*, in which he challenged standard accounts of Southern politics after the Civil War. In response to white historians who argued that black incompetence was responsible for the failure of Republican Reconstruction, Lynch documented black political achievements and the obstacles that African Americans faced. He continued his criticism of historians' work on Reconstruction in essays published in the *Journal of Negro History*.

PUBLICATIONS
The Facts of Reconstruction (1913, reprint 1968)
Reminiscences of an Active Life: The Autobiography of John Roy Lynch (published posthumously in 1970)

FURTHER READING

Foner, Eric. *Freedom's Lawmakers: A Directory of Black Officeholders During Reconstruction.* New York: Oxford University Press, 1993.

Franklin, John Hope. "John Roy Lynch: Republican Stalwart from Mississippi," in Howard N. Rabinowitz, ed., *Southern Black Leaders of the Reconstruction Era.* Urbana: University of Illinois Press, 1982.

Smith, Samuel Denny. *The Negro in Congress, 1870–1901.* Chapel Hill: University of North Carolina Press, 1940.

◇ ◇ ◇

Malcolm X
(el-Hajj Malik el-Shabazz)

NATION OF ISLAM LEADER, BLACK NATIONALIST

Born: May 19, 1925
Omaha, Nebraska

Died: February 21, 1965
New York, New York

Born Malcolm Little in Omaha, Nebraska, he experienced violence and racism early in his life. His parents, followers of the early black nationalist leader Marcus Garvey, were constantly harassed by the Ku Klux Klan. His father died when he was young; Malcolm believed he was murdered by whites. After Malcolm's mother suffered a nervous breakdown and was sent to a state mental hospital, he and his siblings became wards of the state. Malcolm later moved to Boston to live with his older sister Ella. There he transformed himself into an urban hipster with the aid of a conk (a processed hairstyle), a zoot suit, and his own unique style of the lindy hop.

Little moved to New York, where he earned money through hustling. Known as "Detroit Red," he made a living from running numbers, selling drugs, and robbery. He joined many others who participated in the underground economy as their sole source of income or in addition to wage labor. At the age of 20 Little was arrested for burglary and imprisoned.

In prison, Malcolm was introduced to the Nation of Islam and its leader Elijah Muhammad. He took advantage of the prison library and read voraciously. After his release in 1952, Malcolm changed his last name to X and worked his way through the ranks of the Nation of Islam; two years later he was placed in charge of Harlem's Temple Number 7. Malcolm also founded *Muhammad Speaks,* the Nation of Islam's newspaper.

Malcolm was a faithful servant of the Nation and Elijah Muhammad for 12 years, espousing the importance of economic independence and a proud black identity. But his faith began to waver as Malcolm began to believe in the importance of political involvement, which Muhammad forbade, and as he learned about Muhammad's extramarital affairs. He left the Nation in 1964 and started two organizations, the Muslim Mosque, Inc., and the Organization of Afro-American Unity. Malcolm X changed his name to el-Hajj Malik el-Shabazz after making a hajj, or pilgrimage, to Mecca in Saudi Arabia. Malcolm X inspired followers with his fearlessness, wit, and intellect. Using Harlem as his base, Malcolm X spoke out against the aims of the civil rights movement and linked the struggle of blacks in the United States to the issue of human rights worldwide.

Less than a year after his departure from the Nation of Islam and the birth of his organizations, el-Hajj Malik el-Shabazz was murdered at the Audubon Ballroom in Harlem.

PUBLICATIONS
The Autobiography of Malcolm X (with Alex Haley, 1965)
Malcolm X Talks to Young People (1969)

FURTHER READING
Myers, Walter Dean. *Malcolm X: By Any Means Necessary.* New York: Scholastic, 1993.
Rummel, Jack. *Malcolm X.* New York: Chelsea House, 1989.
Wood, Joe, ed. *Malcolm X: In Our Own Image.* New York: St. Martin's, 1992.

Marshall, Thurgood
LAWYER, ACTIVIST, SUPREME COURT JUSTICE

Born: July 2, 1902
Baltimore, Maryland

Died: January 24, 1993
Bethesda, Maryland

Thurgood Marshall grew up in Baltimore with his mother, who was a schoolteacher, and his father, who worked as a steward at a white country club. Denied admission to law school at the University of Maryland because he was black, Marshall entered Howard Law School in 1930. Here he met Charles Hamilton Houston, a black professor of law who was encouraging his students to consider constitutional law as a means of shaping public policy.

Working with Houston, Marshall won his first major victory in an antidiscrimination case in 1935 against the University of Maryland. The following year he moved to New York City to work as legal counsel for the

NAACP. Throughout the late 1930s and 1940s, Marshall, Houston, and other NAACP lawyers focused on litigation that would force federal courts to consider the social and economic effects of segregation and discrimination. In a series of important cases, they challenged discrimination in transportation, employment, universities, professional schools, and housing, each time demonstrating how "separate but equal" facilities or employment discrimination denied blacks equal access to economic and social opportunities.

In case after case, Marshall and his colleagues pressed the courts to clearly define the equal protection clause of the 14th Amendment, a clause that had been severely compromised by the Supreme Court's 1896 ruling in *Plessy* v. *Ferguson.* In a case that would mark a turning point in American law and society, they successfully defended Linda Brown, a black elementary school student in Topeka, Kansas, who was forced to travel miles out of her way each day to attend a segregated facility. In the decision for *Brown* v. *Board of Education* (1954), the Court ruled that education was a "fundamental right. . . that must be protected by the 14th Amendment."

The Brown decision had a momentous impact. Many civil rights activists saw the decision as partial vindication of their struggles and used the precedent to justify their campaigns against other forms of discrimination. Moreover, Marshall's argument and the Court's decision in *Brown* v. *Board of Education* provided important precedents for subsequent legal assaults on segregation and for federal civil rights legislation (most notably the 1964 Voting Rights Act).

Marshall was rightfully acknowledged as one of the critical forces behind this legal revolution, and thereafter became a prominent defender of civil rights. In 1961, President Kennedy appointed him to the U.S. Court of Appeals. In 1965, President Johnson asked Marshall to serve as U.S. Solicitor General, and then four years later appointed him to the U.S. Supreme Court. He was the first African American to serve as a Supreme Court Justice. Until retiring in 1991, Marshall eloquently argued that the federal government should take an active role in protecting its citizens' civil rights.

FURTHER READING

Aldred, Lisa. *Thurgood Marshall.* New York: Chelsea House, 1990.

Rowan, Carl Thomas. *Dream Makers, Dream Breakers: The World of Justice Thurgood Marshall.* Boston: Little, Brown, 1993.

Tushnet, Mark V. *Making Civil Rights Law: Thurgood Marshall and the Supreme Court, 1936–1961.* New York: Oxford University Press, 1994.

McKay, Claude

WRITER, POLITICAL ACTIVIST

Born: September 15, 1889
Clarendon Hills, Jamaica

Died: May 22, 1948
Chicago, Illinois

"All my life I have been a troubadour wanderer, nourishing myself mainly on the poetry of existence. And all I offer here is the distilled poetry of my experience." Claude McKay, poet and novelist, wrote to understand and explain his place in the world. As an immigrant to the United States from Jamaica, he had a mixed relationship with his new home; themes of longing and belonging are found throughout his fiction. Mainly known as a Harlem Renaissance writer, McKay was also very active politically and lived in Europe for more than 10 years.

McKay was born Festus Claudius McKay. At the age of six, he began living with his older brother, Uriah Theophilus, a school-teacher. Uriah encouraged free thinking, which was contrary to the family's strict Catholic upbringing. McKay was also inspired by his encounter with Walter Jekyll, a white Englishman who went to Jamaica to study the island's culture. In 1912, before leaving Jamaica for the United States, McKay published *Songs of Jamaica* and *Constab Ballads,* two volumes of dialect poetry.

After studying at Tuskegee Institute and Kansas State College, McKay moved to New York City to pursue his writing. His first publications appeared in radical and bohemian literary journals. One of McKay's most famous sonnets, "If We Must Die," appeared in the 1919 issue of *The Liberator.* Written in response to race riots that took place throughout the country, this poem became a kind of anthem for blacks and other groups about the importance of dying with dignity and in struggle.

McKay went to the Soviet Union in 1922 to witness communism firsthand, then traveled throughout Europe. It was in Europe that McKay wrote his books on Harlem. With *Harlem Shadows,* McKay came to be seen by many as the best poet since Paul Laurence Dunbar. His first novel, *Home to Harlem,* made a significant break with earlier writers by exploring lower-class black life and offering pimps, prostitutes, and alcoholics as central characters.

McKay returned to the United States in 1934. He found a very different country from the one he had known 12 years before. The Negro Renaissance was over and editors were no longer interested in publishing his work. He was forced to move into a city-operated camp for destitute men in upstate New York. With the help of friends, McKay returned to New York City and began to work on his autobiography, *A Long Way from Home.*

During the 1940s, McKay's health worsened. He moved to Chicago in 1944. Despite frequent hospitalization over the next four years, McKay managed to teach at the Catholic Youth Organization in Chicago and compile his *Selected Poems,* which appeared posthumously in 1953.

FURTHER READING
Cooper, Wayne F. *Claude McKay, Rebel Sojourner in the Harlem Renaissance: A Biography.* Baton Rouge: Louisiana State University Press, 1987.

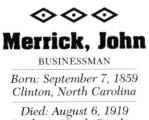

Merrick, John
BUSINESSMAN

Born: September 7, 1859
Clinton, North Carolina

Died: August 6, 1919
Durham, North Carolina

John Merrick was one of the leading businessmen of the South during the first decades of the 20th century. He was part of a new black middle class that contributed to the industrial and economic growth of Durham, North Carolina, the pride of the New South. Nationwide, the black business movement served as a foundation for the New Negro philosophy of economic self-reliance.

Merrick, who was born enslaved, lived most of his life in North Carolina. He and his mother moved to Chapel Hill when he was 12 years old. There Merrick worked in a brickyard. When he was 18, both Merricks moved to Raleigh, where John Merrick continued to work as a manual laborer. He encountered his first business opportunity—learning the barbering trade—while working as a shoeshine boy in a barbershop. In 1880 he moved to Durham with John Wright, another barber, after Wright had been informed that Durham was ripe for a new barbershop. When Wright decided to relocate to Washington, D.C., in 1892, Merrick bought the shop and became owner of his first business. Before the end of the decade Merrick owned five barbershops.

Merrick is most known for organizing, along with six other men, the North Carolina Mutual and Provident Association (later named the North Carolina Mutual Life Insurance Company) in 1898. Dr. Aaron Moore and Charles Spaulding, Merrick's partners in numerous ventures, helped to ensure the success of the insurance company. Many African Americans purchased insurance from white companies. But as the white insurers began to deny policies to African Americans in the 1890s and as African Americans became accustomed to black entrepreneurs, North Carolina Mutual thrived. The North Carolina Mutual Life Insurance Company is still in operation, making it one of the oldest black institutions in the country.

By 1919 Merrick had helped establish the Mechanics and Farmers Bank and founded a drug company, a real estate company, and a textile factory. Through the development of factories, banks, and insurance companies, Merrick and his contemporaries provided needed jobs and services to black workers and consumers.

FURTHER READING

Weare, Walter B. *Black Business in the New South: A Social History of the North Carolina Mutual Life Insurance Company.* Urbana: University of Illinois Press, 1973.

Micheaux, Oscar

FILMMAKER, NOVELIST

Born: January 2, 1884
Metropolis, Illinois

Died: March 25, 1951
Charlotte, North Carolina

Oscar Micheaux, who produced more than 30 films and wrote 10 novels, was one of the earliest black independent filmmakers. He sought to counter one-dimensional and racist representations produced by Hollywood and white independent filmmakers. Involved in every aspect of filmmaking—writing, producing, directing, distributing, and promoting—Micheaux was able to make films with few resources.

Micheaux began his career in the arts writing novels. His first novel, *The Conquest: The Story of a Negro Pioneer* (1913), was apparently inspired by his experiences as a homesteader in South Dakota. His first film was based on his third novel, entitled *Homesteader*. He had offered the film rights to *Homesteader* to the owners of the Lincoln Film Company. But after they refused to allow him to be the director, he decided that he would produce the film himself. He established the Micheaux Book and Film Company in 1918 and began an impressively productive career.

Many communities throughout the country were already familiar with Micheaux and his Western Book Supply Company, which he started after the publication of his first novel. He lectured at churches and schools and met with community leaders to sell his books. He used the same strategies to promote his films.

African Americans were avid filmgoers. During the first decade of the 20th century, when the first all-black films were produced, there were slightly more than 100 theaters catering to black moviegoers. By the end of the 1920s, when Micheaux was the reigning filmmaker, more than 700 theaters served black communities nationwide. Whether Westerns, romances, or comedies were playing, blacks flocked to theaters. Micheaux capitalized on their familiarity with Hollywood films by using similar themes and plots with black characters. Most of Micheaux's films have middle-class characters; Micheaux virtually ignored poverty as a theme in his work.

Micheaux struggled throughout his career. Always operating on a low budget, he was nevertheless able to produce a large number of films. His last film, *Betrayal* (1948), based on his novel *The Wind from Nowhere* (1941), was one of the first to appear in major white theaters. He died in 1951 while on a promotional tour. In 1987 a star bearing Micheaux's name was placed on the Hollywood Walk of Fame.

SELECTED FILMS
Within Our Gates (1919)
The Girl from Chicago (1932)
The Notorious Elinor Lee (1940)

PUBLICATIONS
The Conquest: The Story of a Negro Pioneer
 (1913, reprint 1969)
The Case of Mrs. Wingate (1944)

FURTHER READING
Bogle, Donald. *Toms, Coons, Mulattoes,
 Mammies, and Bucks: An Interpretive
 History of Blacks in American Films*. New
 York: Continuum, 1993.

◇ ◇ ◇

Monk, Thelonious Sphere

PIANIST, COMPOSER

*Born: October 10, 1917
Rocky Mount, North Carolina*

*Died: February 17, 1982
Englewood, New Jersey*

When Thelonious Monk was four years old, his family moved from North Carolina to New York City. He grew up in the San Juan Hill district of Manhattan. In the 1930s he started playing piano professionally, at rent parties in New York and on tour with an evangelist. By 1940, Monk was playing piano in the house band at Minton's Playhouse in Harlem. Here he played with some of the most creative innovators in small group jazz, and he left his distinctive imprint on the emerging bebop sound.

By the time Monk made his first studio recording (with the Coleman Hawkins Quartet in 1944), he was well known among jazz musicians and celebrated for his unconventional approaches to harmony and improvisation.

During these years, he was also playing at the Spotlite Club with Dizzy Gillespie's orchestra. Monk began to attract a wider audience after signing with Blue Note Records in 1947. It was on the Blue Note label that he released some of his most famous and influential recordings, including early versions of "Criss Cross," "Ruby, My Dear," and "Straight, No Chaser." In the early 1950s, Monk also recorded with Charlie Parker, Sonny Rollins, Gigi Gryce, Art Blakey, and Miles Davis.

By the mid-1950s Monk had become enormously popular. A historic summer stint at New York's Five Spot, combined with brilliant recordings in the late 1950s, established Monk as a central figure in modern jazz and as one of its most creative and daring innovators. Monk was heavily influenced by the Harlem "school" of stride piano, a style made famous by artists such as James P. Johnson, Willie "the Lion" Smith, Fats Waller, and Art Tatum. Monk's approach to rhythm was especially unusual and had a dramatic impact on his compositions, which are often spare, playful, and idiosyncratic. For years, many of his contemporaries could not make sense of Monk's work and were often convinced that he was simply playing the "wrong" notes. Actually, he was developing a fresh new style in jazz composition, building upon and expanding the language of the jazz tradition.

During the 1960s, Monk played almost exclusively with his own quartet—which at times featured Charlie Rouse, Roy Haynes and Johnny Griffin—and toured in the United States, Europe, Mexico, and Japan. In 1964, Monk became one of the few jazz musicians to ever be featured on the cover of *Time* magazine. After making a series of solo recordings in 1971, he retired from performances and recording, appearing only a handful of times in the mid-1970s.

FURTHER READING
Goldberg, Joe. *Jazz Masters of the Fifties.* New York: Macmillan, 1965.
Williams, Martin. *The Jazz Tradition.* New York: Oxford University Press, 1983.

Moore, Audley "Queen Mother"

POLITICAL ACTIVIST

Born: July 27, 1898
New Iberia, Louisiana

Audley Moore, who has been involved in most of the major black struggles of the 20th century, has been active in politics since she was 20 years old. Through her range of activism—supporting World War I soldiers, joining the Universal Negro Improvement Association, organizing domestic workers, and running for political office—Moore committed herself to improving the lives of black people worldwide.

Moore grew up with her parents and two sisters in Louisiana. Her parents died when she was young, forcing her to raise and support her younger sisters, Eloise and Lorita, when she became a teenager. Moore was unable to finish her formal education, but she did receive training as a Poro hairdresser. (The Poro Company was founded by Annie Turbo Malone, a contemporary of Madam C. J. Walker.)

Moore was one of the few black women members of the Communist party. Her comrades included Claudia Jones and Louise Patterson. Like many other blacks, she became involved with the party because of its efforts on behalf of the Scottsboro Boys, a group of young black men who were unjustly accused of raping a white woman in the 1930s. Most of Moore's activities with the Communist party involved organizing domestic workers and fighting unfair housing practices.

After Moore left the Communist party in 1950, she became one of the leading voices in the Pan-Africanist movement. As a Pan-Africanist, Moore believed that black people all over the world were connected politically and historically. She and her sister Eloise were two of the cofounders of the Universal Association of Ethiopian Women and the Ethiopian Orthodox Church. Moore also led the 1950s struggle for reparations, or financial payments, to descendants of enslaved Africans for the loss of lives during the Middle Passage, enslavement, and their aftermath. She outlined her quest for reparations in a pamphlet entitled, "Why Reparations? Money for Negroes." In 1962 she met with President Kennedy about her cause and a year later formed the Reparations Committee for the Descendants of American Slaves.

Moore was given the honorary title "Queen Mother" during a trip to Africa for the funeral of Kwame Nkrumah, the president of Ghana, in 1972.

FURTHER READING
Bair, Barbara. "Audley 'Queen Mother' Moore." In *Black Women in America: An Historical Encyclopedia,* edited by Darlene Clark Hine. Brooklyn, N.Y.: Carlson, 1993.
Naison, Mark. *Communists in Harlem During the Depression.* Urbana: University of Illinois Press, 1983.

Morrison, Toni

WRITER, EDITOR

Born: February 18, 1931
Lorain, Ohio

Morrison is one of the most prolific writers of the 20th century. The author of six novels, two edited works, one volume of literary criticism, and a play, Morrison has been recognized with numerous awards and honors for her contribution to American letters; in 1993 she was awarded the Nobel Prize for literature, and in 1988 she won the Pulitzer Prize for fiction.

Morrison was born Chloe Anthony Wofford. (She changed her name to Toni in college.) She and her three siblings were raised by parents steeped in black folklore, particularly storytelling and musical expression. Morrison also read widely as a teenager. After graduating from Lorain High School with honors, Morrison attended Howard University in Washington, D.C., where she majored in English and minored in classics and became a member of the Howard University Players, a theatrical troupe. In 1953 she went to Columbia University to study for an M.A. degree in English; her thesis was on the theme of suicide in the works of William Faulkner and Virginia Woolf.

Morrison taught at Texas Southern University and Howard University before she began, in 1968, a 15-year tenure as an editor at Random House, a major book publishing company in New York City. As a senior editor, Morrison was able to push for the publication of works by African Americans, including John McCluskey and Gayl Jones.

Morrison's own writing career began while she was teaching at Howard. In the late 1950s she joined a writing group, which met monthly to critique the members' work. However, she did not begin to write seriously until the mid-1960s. After coming home from her full-time job and after her two children were asleep, Morrison would stay up nights working on her first novel. This book, *The Bluest Eye* (1970), was based on a shorter work she had shared with her Howard writing group about a dark-skinned black girl who wanted blue eyes.

Morrison's contemporaries include Toni Cade Bambara and Alice Walker. All three writers were first published in the early 1970s and helped to produce a wave of literature by black women that coincided with the development of black feminist political organizers.

In addition to her fiction, Morrison has also worked with other artists in collaborative efforts. In 1992 she wrote the lyrics for *Honey and Rue,* an operetta whose premiere featured soprano Kathleen Battle. In 1995 she worked with musician/composer Max Roach and dancer/choreographer Bill T. Jones in a piece entitled *Degga.* Since 1989 Morrison has taught at Princeton University.

SELECTED PUBLICATIONS
Sula (1973)
Song of Solomon (1977)
Tar Baby (1981)
Beloved (1987)

FURTHER READING
Kramer, Barbara. *Toni Morrison: Nobel Prize-winning Author.* Hillside, N.J.: Enslow, 1996.
Peach, Linden. *Toni Morrison.* New York: St. Martin's, 1995.

Overton, Anthony

LAWYER, BUSINESSMAN

Born: March 21, 1865
Monroe, Louisiana

Died: July 3, 1946
Chicago, Illinois

Little is known about Anthony Overton's early life. He probably attended Washburn College in Topeka, Kansas, and earned a law degree from the University of Kansas in 1888. That same year, he married Clara Gregg. After serving as a municipal judge in Topeka for several years, he established Overton's Hygienic Products Company in Kansas City, Kansas. The venture manufactured baking powder, flavor extracts, and toiletries. In 1911 he moved the company to Chicago, where it grew into a million-dollar enterprise, internationally famous for its "High Brown Face Powder" and other cosmetics for African Americans.

Overton used some of his profits to establish new business ventures, including the Victory Life Insurance Company and a South Side weekly newspaper, the *Chicago Bee*. In order to make business and home loans available to more African Americans, he founded the Douglass National Bank in Chicago in 1922. Victory Life, founded two years later, was the first black-owned insurance company permitted to do business in New York. Although neither the bank nor the insurance company survived the Great Depression, Overton continued to lead other companies until his death. Throughout his life, he was an active member of the Chicago Urban League and other social and civic organizations.

Like other black business pioneers of the early 20th century, Overton struggled to set up independent African-American businesses in an economic and political environment that was very hostile to black entrepreneurs. He and other black business owners—such as Madam C. J. Walker, Jesse A. Binga, Maggie Lena Walker, Harry H. Pace, and Philip A. Payton—helped support their communities by providing loans, insurance, services, and employment. And they set important examples for African Americans at a time when relatively few black people had access to economic independence.

FURTHER READING
Poinsett, Alex. "Unsung Black Business Giants," *Ebony*, March 1990.

Owen, Chandler

JOURNALIST, POLITICAL PARTY OFFICIAL

Born: April 5, 1889
Warrenton, North Carolina

Died: 1967
place of death unknown

Chandler Owen was born and raised in the South and graduated from Virginia Union University in 1913. He moved to New York soon thereafter to study at Columbia University on a scholarship from the National Urban League. In New York, Owen met A. Philip Randolph and began to study the work of Karl Marx, Lester Frank, and other radical thinkers.

In 1916 Owen and Randolph joined the Socialist party. After editing a newsletter for black hotel employees, they began publishing a monthly political magazine, *The Messenger*, in 1917. During its first six years of publication, Owen and Randolph used *The Messenger* to publish essays about contemporary racial politics, to educate black readers about the American Socialist party, and to encourage the development of militant labor unions in the United States. *The Messenger* advocated U.S. withdrawal from World War I and urged African Americans to take up arms in self-defense against white lynch mobs. For their efforts, both Owen and Randolph were briefly jailed on charges of espionage and the office of *The Messenger* was repeatedly raided by the police. Soon after leaving *The Messenger* in 1923, Owen became the editor of Anthony Overton's *Chicago Bee*. Although Owen had grown somewhat disenchanted with radical politics by this time, he was one of the few black public figures to support Randolph's efforts to organize a union of railway porters. In Chicago, Owen also turned his attention to mainstream politics. He lost a bid for a seat in the House of Representatives in 1928, but soon became influential in the local Republican party organization. He worked as a political consultant for the party and served as a speechwriter in the Presidential campaigns of Wendell Wilkie, Thomas Dewey, and Dwight Eisenhower.

Owen spent much of his later professional career working in the field of public relations. During World War II, Owen wrote *Negroes and the War,* a widely circulated government pamphlet that encouraged African Americans to support the U.S. war effort. Owen also worked for the Anti-Defamation League of B'nai B'rith. Though he remained a loyal Republican for most of his life, Owen also wrote materials for Democrats and supported Lyndon Johnson in the 1960s.

FURTHER READING
Kornweibel, Theodore Jr. *"No Crystal Stair": Black Life and the Messenger, 1917–1928.* Westport, Conn.: Greenwood, 1975.

◇ ◇ ◇
Parker, Charlie ("Yardbird," "Bird")
SAXOPHONIST, COMPOSER

Born: August 29, 1920
Kansas City, Kansas

Died: March 12, 1955
New York, New York

Charlie Parker's work as a jazz composer and soloist revolutionized American music during the 1940s and 1950s. As a child, Parker was steeped in jazz and the blues. When he was seven years old, his family moved to Kansas City, Missouri, which was at the time an important center of African-American music. After taking lessons on the baritone sax in the public schools Parker taught himself the alto sax at the age of 10 and began to play in local groups. Soon after hearing alto sax great Lester Young play at a local club in 1934, Parker left high school to become a full-time musician. He played Kansas City clubs throughout the late 1930s and in 1939 visited New York City, where he was deeply influenced by artists such as Buster "Prof" Smith and Art Tatum.

Later that year he moved to New York City, where he remained based for most of his professional career. During the early 1940s he performed with big bands led by Jay McShann, Earl Hines, and Billy Eckstine, and participated in small-group, after-hours jam sessions at clubs, including Minton's Playhouse and Monroe's Uptown House. It was in these small-group settings that Parker felt free to explore new approaches to composition and improvisation. Together with innovators such as Dizzy Gillespie, Kenny Clarke, Bud Powell, Thelonious Monk, and Max Roach, Parker helped develop and popularize a style of jazz known as "bebop" (or "bop"). Parker introduced approaches to melody, harmony, and, most fundamentally, to rhythm that changed the ways that many musicians played jazz.

By 1945, Parker was leading his own small group in New York and was working with Dizzy Gillespie on a regular basis. In 1947 Parker formed perhaps his most famous quintet, which included Tommy Potter, Miles Davis, Duke Jordan, and Max Roach. Parker also played with a number of other small groups, with string bands, and with Afro-Cuban groups during the late 1940s. He toured Europe in 1949 and 1950.

Parker was plagued by drug and alcohol addiction throughout his career. Suffering from poor health and deeply in debt, Parker committed himself to Bellevue Hospital in New York in 1954. He performed briefly after his release, but died in 1955 at the age of 34.

He left behind a remarkable legacy. Many of Parker's contemporaries rejected bebop, feeling that it was too radical a departure from music's mainstream. But many others embraced his work, and by the mid-1950s countless artists were playing bop and were further exploring its innovations. Parker's

recordings, made between 1940 and 1955, are regarded today as legendary and are seen as documents of a period of experimentation central to the history of modern jazz. Parker's work continues to influence the ways that musicians compose and perform the music.

FURTHER READING

Frankl, Ron. *Charlie Parker*. New York: Chelsea House, 1993.

Giddins, Gary. *Celebrating Bird: The Life of Charlie Parker*. Morrow, 1986.

Russell, Ross. *Bird Lives: The High Life and Hard Times of Charlie (Yardbird) Parker*. New York: Charterhouse, 1973.

Pickens, William

EDUCATOR, CIVIL RIGHTS ACTIVIST, EDITOR

Born: January 15, 1881
Anderson County, South Carolina

Died: April 6, 1954
Off the coast of Jamaica

William Pickens was one of 10 children born to Jacob and Fannie Pickens, both of whom had been born in slavery. When William was seven years old, the Pickens family moved from South Carolina to Arkansas with the hope of making a living as tenant farmers. Because he had to help his family on the farm, William missed at least a year of school when he was young. Still, he excelled in oratory and literature and graduated first in his class at Little Rock High School in 1899.

Pickens attended Talladega College in Alabama for three years before transferring in 1902 to Yale, where he earned a degree in classics in 1904. He taught at Talladega, at Wiley University in Texas, and at Morgan College in Baltimore while working with a number of black political organizations.

During these years, Pickens established himself as one of the most prominent public speakers in the country. In early speeches he supported the "accommodationist" strategy made famous by Booker T. Washington, but by 1905 Pickens was endorsing political strategies aimed at ensuring equality for African Americans. Pickens worked with the NAACP on some of its earliest civil rights campaigns and helped establish a branch office in Louisville, Kentucky, before leaving Morgan College in 1920 to work full time for the organization. During his more than 20 years of service with the NAACP, Pickens helped expand and administer branch operations, raised money, and investigated lynchings and discrimination in the South. Pickens described his early years of teaching and activism in an autobiography, *Bursting Bonds,* published in 1929.

Pickens was often critical of the NAACP's political strategies and the organization's cooperation with radical political groups like the Communist party. During World War II, while working in the Bonds Division of the U.S. Treasury Department, he criticized the NAACP's campaign against segregation in the armed forces. Pickens came under fire throughout the black community, and the NAACP dismissed him as field secretary in 1942. At the Treasury Department, Pickens helped raise more than a billion dollars for the U.S. war effort. He retired in 1950.

PUBLICATION
Bursting Bonds (1929)

FURTHER READING
Avery, Sheldon. *Up from Washington: William Pickens and the Negro Struggle for Equality, 1900–1954.* Newark: University of Delaware Press, 1989.

Poitier, Sidney
ACTOR, DIRECTOR, PRODUCER
*Born: February 20, 1927
Miami, Florida*

Sidney Poitier was raised on Cat Island in the Bahamas. He left school at 15 to work on his family's farm, then moved to New York City. After serving in the army during World War II, he returned to New York and worked a variety of jobs. He responded to a newspaper ad for auditions at the American Negro Theater (ANT) but was rejected. After training himself to "lose" his West Indian accent, Poitier was accepted by the ANT as a student in 1946.

He starred in a number of ANT productions and played some minor parts in Broadway plays before making his Hollywood debut in *No Way Out* (1950), the first of a series of postwar movies exploring racism and other social problems in the United States. A number of leading roles followed, making him one of the most widely recognized African-American artists of the decade and one of the most celebrated black actors of his generation.

For his performance in *The Defiant Ones* (1958), Poitier received international acclaim and became the first African American nominated in the category of Best Actor at the Academy Awards. He starred on Broadway in *A Raisin in the Sun* (1959) and in films including *Porgy and Bess* (1959), *Lilies of the Field* (1963), and *In the Heat of the Night* (1967). For his performance in *Lilies of the Field*, he became the first African American to win an Academy Award for Best Actor.

Poitier's work has long been at the center of controversy. Many critics argued that audiences were attracted to him in part because he played "respectable," "integrationist" characters—characters who lived by white, middle-class standards and who thus posed no threat to the racial status quo. By the late 1960s, Poitier tried to respond to the mounting criticism by taking on film roles that were more controversial.

He also turned to film production and direction. He joined other prominent artists in forming an independent production company in 1978, and directed several commercially successful comedies. He returned to acting in the late 1980s.

PUBLICATION
This Life (1980)

FURTHER READING
Bergman, Carol. *Sidney Poitier.* New York: Chelsea House, 1988.
Cripps, Thomas. *Making Movies Black: The Hollywood Message Movie from World War II to the Civil Rights Era.* New York: Oxford University Press, 1993.

Randolph, Asa Philip

PUBLICIST, LABOR LEADER, ACTIVIST

Born: April 15, 1889
Crescent City, Florida

Died: May 16, 1979
New York, New York

Growing up in a comfortable middle-class home, A. Philip Randolph first studied with private tutors, then attended the Cookman Institute in Jacksonville, Florida. He moved to New York City in 1911 and like

many middle-class, educated black men, found work as a Pullman porter.

While attending City College in New York, Randolph became involved in union organizing and socialist politics. With Chandler Owen, Randolph founded *The Messenger* in 1917. Proclaiming itself the "Only Radical Negro Magazine in America," *The Messenger* quickly became a rallying point for many politically outspoken African Americans. The editors encouraged blacks to own weapons so that they could defend themselves against lynchings. After Randolph publicly declared his opposition to black participation in World War I, U.S. Attorney General Mitchell Palmer labeled him the "most dangerous Negro in America."

In 1925 the Pullman porters of New York City recruited Randolph to spearhead their latest attempt to organize a union, and the Brotherhood of Sleeping Car Porters (BSCP) was founded that year at a meeting in Harlem. *The Messenger* became its official publication, and the BSCP quickly became a national symbol of the "New Negro." Randolph and his colleagues used the magazine and the union campaign to link debates over black civil rights to the issues of work and economic equality.

White union members and the Pullman Company resisted black unionization, and many prominent black journalists attacked the efforts of the BSCP. Finally, after years of strikes and publicity campaigns, and after President Roosevelt pushed through Congress legislation that protected the right of all workers to unionize, the Brotherhood won Pullman's recognition in 1937. The BSCP did not have a large membership, but its victory had enormous symbolic significance nationwide for black working people, most of whom had closely followed the union's struggles for more than a decade in the black press.

Randolph used his position as a prominent activist and spokesman to support early civil rights struggles. In 1941, he helped plan the first March on Washington. Although the march was eventually called off, the plans forced Roosevelt to sign legislation that required companies with federal contracts to hire black workers. When Randolph threatened to call a black boycott of the military draft, President Truman decreed the end of segregation of the armed forces in July 1948. In the 1950s, Randolph continued his labor and civil rights work and campaigned for the integration of schools. At the age of 74, he served as chairman of the 1963 March on Washington.

FURTHER READING

Harris, William H. *Keeping the Faith: A. Philip Randolph, Milton P. Webster, and the Brotherhood of Sleeping Car Porters, 1925–1937*. Urbana: University of Illinois Press, 1977.

Pfeffer, Paula. *A. Philip Randolph: Pioneer of the Civil Rights Movement*. Baton Rouge: Louisiana State University Press, 1990.

Wright, Sarah E. *A. Philip Randolph*. Englewood Cliffs, N.J.: Silver Burdett, 1990.

Ransom, Reverdy Cassius

BISHOP, CIVIL RIGHTS LEADER, EDITOR

*Born: January 1 or 4, 1861
Flushing, Ohio*

*Died: April 22, 1959
Wilberforce, Ohio*

Reverdy Cassius Ransom was a leader in the African Methodist Episcopal church for more than 40 years. As a bishop, journal editor, and lecturer, Ransom spurred the growth of the A.M.E. church and built relationships with other black Christians.

Ransom lived most of his young life in various cities throughout Ohio. His first association with the A.M.E. church began when he was a child; the school he attended was held in an A.M.E. building. The association continued when he enrolled at Wilberforce University in Wilberforce, Ohio, in 1881. Wilberforce, founded by the A.M.E. church at the insistence of bishop Daniel A. Payne, was the first college started by African Americans. After one year at Oberlin College, Ohio, Ransom returned to Wilberforce, graduating from the theological department in 1886.

Soon after graduation, Ransom began his life work as pastor to A.M.E. congregations throughout the United States. In several of these churches, Ransom instituted social welfare programs for the members. While in Chicago, he established the Institutional Church and Social Settlement in 1900. Working with Jane Addams, a leader in the white settlement house movement and founder of Hull House, Ransom sought to provide support to the thousands of Southern migrants to Chicago. The Institutional Church provided a gymnasium, reading rooms, and a school to this community. Ransom also founded the Men's Sunday Club, a social organization.

Ransom was next a pastor in Boston and New York. In New York, he served as editor of the *A.M.E. Review,* one of the church's publications. In 1934 Ransom helped found the Fraternal Council of Negro Churches, which brought together leaders of various black denominations. He also served as chairman of the board of trustees at Wilberforce University. In addition, he wrote six books, including an autobiography, *The Pilgrimage of Harriet Ransom's Son*.

FURTHER READING
Morris, Calvin S. *Reverdy C. Ransom: Black Advocate of the Social Gospel.* Lanham, Md.: University Press of America, 1990.

Robeson, Paul
ACTOR, SINGER, ACTIVIST

*Born: April 9, 1898
Princeton, New Jersey*

*Died: January 23, 1976
Philadelphia, Pennsylvania*

Paul Robeson pursued his many interests and demonstrated his many talents from an early age. The son of a former slave, Robeson attended the predominantly white public schools of Princeton and Somerville, New Jersey, and then Rutgers College. He excelled in his academic work, on sports teams, in debate, and in musical and theatrical productions. At Somerville High he presented his first Shakespearean monologues. At Rutgers he was a football all-American. In his graduation speeches the young Robeson invoked Toussaint Louverture and made calls for "racial progress."

After graduating as valedictorian of Rutgers' class of 1919, Robeson moved to Harlem and attended the Columbia University Law School, supporting himself with acting jobs and by playing professional football on the weekends. He earned a law degree in 1923 and joined a

New York firm, but quickly left it to pursue a career in stage acting.

Robeson became an immediate success in the 1923 production of *The Emperor Jones,* followed in 1925 by his role in *All God's Chillun Got Wings*. That same year, he performed a concert of African-American spirituals with pianist Lawrence Brown in New York City. For much of the next three decades, his interpretations of dramatic roles, his musical performances, and his film acting were legendary both in the United States and abroad. His highly acclaimed performance in an English production of *Showboat* (1928) was later revived in the United States, and his confident, assertive acting style redeemed a number of otherwise demeaning film roles. Robeson's interpretation of Othello (on Broadway beginning in 1943) is regarded as one of the finest ever performed.

During the 1930s, Robeson became increasingly involved in radical politics. His frustration with white racism in the United States and his popularity in the Soviet Union (following his first visit in 1934) helped attract Robeson to radical socialism. Robeson became a vocal supporter of liberal causes throughout the world, including the anti-colonial movement in Africa. As a result, most whites and eventually most blacks distanced themselves from him, and he quickly became a target of anti-communist hysteria after World War II. When Robeson asserted in 1949 that African Americans should not support U.S. troops if war were declared against the Soviet Union, the State Department revoked his passport. When Robeson refused to renounce his support for communism, his illustrious performance career came to an end.

In the late 1950s, Robeson was able to tour briefly in the United States, but he soon returned to the Soviet Union. His health deteriorating, he moved back to Harlem in 1963 and then lived in Philadelphia with his sister. In 1973, more than two decades after being blacklisted and persecuted for his political convictions, the same artistic communities that ostracized Robeson honored him with a tribute at Carnegie Hall.

PUBLICATION
Here I Stand (1971)

FURTHER READING
Duberman, Martin. *Paul Robeson.* New York: Knopf, 1989.
Ehrlich, Scott. *Paul Robeson.* New York: Chelsea House, 1989.

Smith, Bessie
SINGER, SONGWRITER

Born: April 15, 1894
Chattanooga, Tennessee

Died: September 26, 1937
Clarksdale, Mississippi

Bessie Smith was the most popular and one of the most influential blues artists of the 1920s. She grew up in extreme poverty in Chattanooga, the youngest of seven children born to William and Laura Smith. The family's living conditions were so severe that Bessie's parents and two of her siblings died before she reached the age of nine. To earn money, Bessie sang and danced on street corners, accompanied on guitar by her brother Andrew.

After winning local amateur contests, Smith joined a traveling vaudeville troupe as a dancer in 1912, and later performed with a troupe in Dalton, Georgia. Within a year she moved to Atlanta, where she sang regularly at Charles Bailey's 81 Theater.

She also began touring the East Coast and the South, singing at a circuit of venues affiliated with the Theater Owners Booking Association (TOBA). Smith's magnetic performances of blues standards earned her a loyal following, making her a headliner in cities throughout these regions by 1918. In 1921 and 1922 she performed regularly with her own band in Philadelphia and Atlantic City. Despite her popularity, however, Smith reaped little financial reward from her work; the managers of TOBA clubs barely paid their black performers and subjected them to horrendous working conditions.

Smith's music was especially popular with blacks in the rural South, and with blacks who had recently migrated from the countryside to the city. Her lyrics were drawn from the African-American oral tradition, and her rich, distinctive voice spoke passionately to black audiences about struggles familiar to many of them. Smith sang about everyday struggles facing black people, and especially black women, in songs about work, life in the city, injustice, sexuality, prison, and poverty.

Smith's rise to prominence coincided with record companies' discovery that they could successfully market recordings of black artists to black audiences. Despite her reputation and popularity, several record companies refused to record Smith, believing that her music sounded too rural, too "rough," or too "black" to be marketable. When Columbia Records finally signed Smith in 1923, her version of "Down Hearted Blues" sold over 780,000 copies in just six months.

Smith recorded constantly for the next six years, with jazz artists including Fletcher Henderson, Clarence Williams, and James P. Johnson. Through recordings and performances, Smith and other black women blues singers introduced artists and audiences to new styles of singing and melody, and influenced the ways that blues and jazz musicians interpreted traditional material.

By 1929 sales of recordings by black women singers had dropped off, leading Columbia to drop Smith from its label. She attempted to change her style to suit public tastes, but never regained the popularity of her earlier blues career. Smith was killed in an automobile accident while on tour in the South in 1937.

FURTHER READING

Albertson, Chris. *Bessie Smith: Empress of the Blues*. New York: Schirmer, 1975.
Harrison, Daphne Duval. *Black Pearls: Blues Queens of the 1920s*. New Brunswick, N.J.: Rutgers University Press, 1988.

Smith, Mamie

SINGER

Born: May 26, 1883
Cincinnati, Ohio

Died: October 30, 1946
New York, New York

Little is known about Mamie Smith's childhood. As a child and teenager, she performed with a number of vaudeville troupes, including the Four Dancing Mitchells and Tutt

Whitney's Smart Set Company, a black minstrel troupe. After marrying William "Smitty" Smith in 1912 and moving to New York, she gained a local following by singing in Harlem clubs and theaters.

In 1918 she was hired to perform in *Made in Harlem*, a production staged by Perry Bradford. At a time when record companies were reluctant to record black artists, Bradford convinced Okeh Records to record Smith singing "That Thing Called Love" and "You Can't Keep a Good Man Down" in 1920. These were some of the earliest recordings made by an African-American singer. When the songs sold well, Okeh agreed to record Smith singing Bradford's "Crazy Blues," which many consider to be the first blues recording. "Crazy Blues" sold more than a million copies, demonstrating to record executives that there was an enormous market for the work of black musicians and vocalists. Though Smith's singing was more heavily influenced by vaudeville than by the blues, her success helped pave the way for dozens of black women blues singers, including Ma Rainey and Bessie Smith.

The success of "Crazy Blues" quickly made Smith one of the most widely recognized entertainers in the nation. Throughout the 1920s and 1930s she toured the country, working with some of the most influential blues and jazz artists of the time, including Coleman Hawkins and Sidney Bechet. For many of her recordings and performances she was backed by her own group, the Jazz Hounds, whose personnel included pianist Fats Waller and trumpeter Johnny Dunn. She performed in a variety of stage shows and, beginning in 1929, appeared in short films and feature-length movies.

Smith recorded steadily, mostly for Okeh Records, until the market for "race records" collapsed in the early 1930s. Thereafter, she continued to star in popular jazz and blues films, including *Paradise in Harlem* (1939) and *Murder on Lenox Avenue* (1941).

FURTHER READING
Harrison, Daphne Duval. *Black Pearls: Blues Queens of the 1920s.* New Brunswick, N.J.: Rutgers University Press, 1988.

❖ ❖ ❖
Stewart, Maria W.
WOMEN'S RIGHTS ACTIVIST, JOURNALIST, EDUCATOR

Born: 1803
Hartford, Connecticut

Died: December 17, 1879
Washington, D.C.

Maria W. Stewart, the first American-born woman to present a public political speech to an audience of women and men, used a number of media to express her views on women's rights and racial justice. Besides lecturing, she also wrote essays and poems. Stewart was outspoken at a time when it was deemed inappropriate for women to engage in political discussions. Although often rebuffed by blacks and whites, Stewart was steadfast in her right to protest injustice.

Stewart was born free in 1803 and orphaned at the age of five. As a teenager, she worked as a domestic servant while attending school. She moved to Boston as an adult and became part of Boston's small but significant black middle class. Stewart was inspired by a fellow Boston-

ian, David Walker, whose *Appeal to the Colored Citizens of the World* (1829) advocated that blacks defend themselves against white repression and become more politically aggressive.

Stewart's first publication, *Religion and the Pure Principles of Morality, the Sure Foundation on Which We Must Build,* was published in 1831 by William Lloyd Garrison, editor of *The Liberator,* an abolitionist weekly. Four years later, Garrison published *Productions of Mrs. Maria W. Stewart,* a volume of collected works that includes texts of four public speeches, biographical facts, essays, and poems. Stewart's last work, a book of religious pieces, *Meditations from the Pen of Mrs. Maria W. Stewart,* was published in 1879.

Stewart gave her first speech in 1832 to the African-American Female Intelligence Society of America. In this speech, she spoke out against the colonization movement, a scheme to return blacks to Africa. Her second lecture, the first ever given in the United States to a public meeting of men and women, was presented in the same year. She gave two final speeches in 1833 at the African Masonic Hall and at the African Meeting House. The African Meeting House was particularly appropriate for her *Farewell Address* because the New England Anti-Slavery Society had been started there in 1832.

Stewart spent several years in New York and Baltimore before she settled in Washington, D.C., in the early 1860s. She continued to teach, and in 1871 opened a Sunday school for children.

FURTHER READING
Richardson, Marilyn. *Maria W. Stewart, America's First Black Woman Political Writer: Essays and Speeches.* Bloomington: Indiana University Press, 1987.

Stokes, Carl Burton

LAWYER, POLITICIAN

Born: June 21, 1927
Cleveland, Ohio

Died: April 3, 1996
Cleveland, Ohio

Carl Stokes was raised in Cleveland by his mother, who worked as a domestic, and by his grandmother (his father died when Carl was young). At age 17 he dropped out of high school and tried to make a living shooting pool. After a stint in the army, he earned a high school diploma, then attended colleges in Virginia, Ohio, and Minnesota. He also worked for the Ohio State Department of Liquor Control and as a probation officer while studying law at night. In 1956 he earned a law degree from Cleveland State University and opened a law firm with his brother.

Two years later Stokes began his career of public service when Cleveland's Democratic mayor asked him to serve as assistant city prosecutor. Stokes was also active in local civil rights politics and was eventually elected to the executive committee of the Cleveland NAACP. In 1962 he became the first black Democrat elected to Ohio's general assembly.

Stokes ran for mayor in 1965 and lost the election by a slim margin. In 1967, after aggressive voter registration drives by black activists expanded the electoral base in Cleveland's African-American wards, he was elected mayor. He and Richard Hatcher of Gary, Indiana, were the first African Americans to be elected mayors of major American cities.

During his two terms of office, Stokes concentrated on improving Cleveland's school system, expanding basic city services, building public housing, and securing funds to support small and minority-owned businesses. Through his "Cleveland: NOW!" initiative, he encouraged citizens to participate in youth and neighborhood renewal programs.

In the summer of 1968, Stokes became the target of harsh criticism from both black and white supporters, who were upset by his responses to a violent clash between black nationalists and the Cleveland police. Many voters were also losing patience with Stokes's proposals to raise income taxes further. Sensing that he had lost the white electoral support crucial to his two previous victories, Stokes chose not to run for a third term.

In 1972 he moved to New York City, where he anchored a local television news program. In 1980 he returned to Cleveland to practice law and three years later was elected a municipal court judge.

PUBLICATION
Promises of Power (1973)

FURTHER READING
Weinberg, Kenneth G. *Black Victory: Carl Stokes and the Winning of Cleveland.* Chicago: Quadrangle, 1968.

Tarry, Ellen

AUTHOR, JOURNALIST, SOCIAL WORKER

Born: September 26, 1906
Birmingham, Alabama

Ellen Tarry was born and raised in Birmingham, Alabama, in a comfortable, middle-class home. Her mother, Eula Meadows, worked as a seamstress, and her father, John Tarry, worked as a barber. Ellen first demonstrated her talents as a writer when she was a student at the Slater Elementary School. In 1921, she moved to Rock Castle, Virginia, to attend a Catholic boarding school, the St. Francis de Sales Institute. Tarry had been brought up in the Methodist Episcopal church, then joined the Congregational church at the age of 12. By the time she graduated from St. Francis in 1923, she had converted to Catholicism.

At the Alabama State Normal School (later Alabama State College), Tarry trained for a career in teaching. After earning her college degree, she worked as a substitute teacher in Birmingham and taught classes for adults at the Knights of Columbus Evening School. Between 1925 and 1929, Tarry taught the fourth and fifth grades at her alma mater, the Slater School. With the help of local librarians, Tarry collected as much information as she could about famous black men and women and wrote biographies that she then taught to her fifth-grade students.

Tarry continued to work on her writing. The biographies that she assembled for her students became the basis for "Negroes of Note," a regular column that Tarry wrote for *The Birmingham Truth*. She also contributed outspoken editorials that condemned racial discrimination. In 1929, Tarry moved to New York City. Unable to find work in her field, she kept a series of poorly paid jobs for several years. She eventually joined the Writers Workshop at Bank Street College. In the mid-1930s, as a member of the Negro Writers'

Guild, Tarry befriended Claude McKay, Sterling Brown, James Weldon Johnson, and other talented journalists and fiction writers.

Tarry's activities in the 1930s and 1940s demonstrate the breadth of her interests, talents and commitments. She worked for the Federal Writers Project in 1936 and attended the Cooperative School for Student Teachers in 1936–37. For many years she worked with Friendship House, a white-run Catholic center in Harlem. She later did social service work with the Catholic church in Chicago, New York City, and Orangeburg, New Jersey. After working with the National Catholic Community Service–USO in Alabama, Tarry supervised the Harlem Area National Catholic Council and helped establish a Catholic community center there in the early 1950s. Tarry was a journalist for the *Amsterdam News* and contributed articles to *Catholic World* and *Commonweal*. She published several books for children, including *Jannie Bell* (1940) and *Runaway Elephant* (1950). Her book *My Dog Rinty* (1946) was popular for its portrayal of Harlem in the 1940s. In her autobiography, *The Third Door* (1955), Tarry explores her racial identity and her childhood in the South.

In 1958, Tarry was hired as an adviser for the U.S. Housing and Home Finance Agency (HHFA). She later worked as an intergroup relations specialist for the HHFA and for its successor, the U.S. Department of Housing and Urban Development. Tarry lives in New York City.

SELECTED PUBLICATIONS
Jannie Bell (1940)
My Dog Rinty (1946)
The Third Door (1955, reprint 1992)

Terrell, Mary Church

CIVIL RIGHTS LEADER, CLUBWOMAN

Born: September 23, 1863
Memphis, Tennessee

Died: July 24, 1954
Washington, D.C.

Mary Church Terrell was a major leader in civil rights for more than six decades. As cofounder and president of the National Association of Colored Women, Terrell worked with hundreds of other women to fight against race and gender oppression. Terrell also spearheaded civil rights demonstrations in Washington, D.C., in the 1950s, predating activism by college students in the South in the early 1960s.

Mary Eliza Church, nicknamed Mollie, spent her childhood in Memphis, Tennessee, New York, and Ohio. After her parents separated in 1869, she and her mother moved to New York, where her mother operated a hair salon. Her mother sent her to a unique integrated school in Ohio with hopes that she would receive a better education there than in the segregated schools in New York. She stayed in Ohio to attend Oberlin College, where she and two other students became the first black women graduates in 1884. After teaching one year at Wilberforce University, she moved to Washington, D.C., to teach at M Street High School.

Terrell immersed herself in local, national, and international politics. She became the first woman member of the District of Columbia Board of Education. In 1896 the National Association of Colored Women (NACW) was formed, and Terrell was elected the first president. The NACW is one of the earliest modern national civil rights organizations, predating the National Association for the Advancement of Colored People and the National Urban League. Formed from regional black women's clubs, the NACW organized around numerous issues, including suffrage, temperance, and education. In 1904 Terrell, who spoke three languages, addressed the International Congress of Women in Berlin. She delivered her lecture about black politics in the United States in German.

Terrell was also a popular lecturer and writer in the United States. The major themes in her speeches in the first decades of the twentieth century were interracial understanding and racial pride. In her numerous articles she wrote biographies of accomplished blacks, as well as essays on lynching and the penal system. Terrell also wrote short stories using materials from her magazine articles.

During World War I, Terrell worked as a clerk for several government agencies. In 1934, she returned to her work as a clerk for a government agency, but was fired, allegedly because of an agency restructuring. Frustrated by what she considered to be racial discrimination, Terrell devoted most of her time and energy to her autobiography, which she had begun writing in 1927.

After her autobiography was published in 1940, Terrell returned to political organizing with zeal. She adopted a more activist stance: her strategy shifted to addressing unjust laws in the courts and direct-action protests. In February 1950 Terrell and three other activists—two black and one white—staged a sit-in at a restaurant that practiced segregation. Although segregation was not established by law in Washington, D.C., black residents understood that most white establishments—such as restaurants, theaters, and department stores—did not welcome their business. Their fight was successful. Three years after the protests began, segregation at eating establishments was deemed unconstitutional.

PUBLICATION
A Colored Woman in a White World (1940)

FURTHER READING
Shaw, Stephanie J. *What a Woman Ought to Be and Do: Black Professional Women Workers During the Jim Crow Era.* Chicago: University of Chicago Press, 1996.

Sterling, Dorothy. *Black Foremothers: Three Lives.* 2nd ed. New York: Feminist Press, 1988.

Washington, Beverly Jones. *Quest for Equality: The Life and Writings of Mary Church Terrell, 1863–1954.* Brooklyn, N.Y.: Carlson, 1990.

Terrell, Robert H.

LAWYER, JUDGE

Born: November 25, 1857
Orange County, Virginia

Died: December 19, 1925
Washington, D.C.

Robert H. Terrell, a municipal judge for more than 20 years, was part of an elite group of African Americans who were financially successful and well educated. Terrell and his wife Mary Church Terrell were part of Washington, D.C.'s, privileged class. This group created its own institutions and societies, but also moved in white circles and had access to the White House.

Terrell was raised in Washington, D.C., by his formerly enslaved parents, Louise Coleman and William Henry Harrison Terrell. It is believed that his father served as a personal servant to President Ulysses S. Grant and to Washington banker John Riggs. Terrell was fortunate enough to receive an excellent education. He attended the Preparatory High School in Washington, D.C., Lawrence Academy in Groton, Massachusetts, Harvard College, and Howard University. At Lawrence Academy, Terrell received the highest prize in oratory. Terrell also excelled at Harvard, where he graduated with honors and was selected as one of the five commencement speakers in 1884. His speech was entitled "The Negro Race in America Since Its Emancipation." After graduation, Terrell returned to Washington, D.C., to teach in the public school system. At the same time, he worked on a law degree at Howard University. He was the class valedictorian in 1889 and four years later received a master's degree in law.

Terrell started a law practice with John Roy Lynch, a former Reconstruction congressman. After the practice dissolved, Terrell returned to the public school system from 1899 to 1901, serving as president of the M Street High School. At the end of his tenure he was appointed justice of the peace by President Theodore Roosevelt. In 1902, Terrell was appointed to the Washington, D.C., Municipal Court, making him the first African American in this position. He was revered for his brilliance and mild manner. A property case that Terrell decided on, *Block* v. *Hirsh* (1920), was appealed to the U.S. Supreme Court, which upheld Terrell's decision. This was widely hailed in the black press. Terrell served six consecutive terms as a judge.

Politically, Terrell aligned himself with Booker T. Washington (who was partly responsible for his appointment). In his lectures, Terrell urged blacks to remain with the Republican party. Despite his liberal arts education, Terrell was a strong advocate of industrial education. He also advocated a conservative approach to race relations, preferring to write letters to members of Congress, urging them to address injustice. At the same time, Terrell was an ardent supporter of woman suffrage; in his lectures, he implored men to work with women to obtain voting rights for women.

Toomer, Jean

WRITER

Born: December 26, 1894
Washington, D.C.

Died: March 30, 1967
Bucks County, Pennsylvania

Jean Toomer, author of *Cane*, a novel considered one of the best works of fiction from the Harlem Renaissance, spent much of his life rejecting the term "black writer." As the racial classifications of black and white became solidified by 1920, Toomer promoted the idea of one American race. His rejection of the idea of racial categories stemmed partly from his claim that the only "black blood" he had came from one of his grandfathers who was "barely black." Toomer was very light-skinned and could have easily "passed" for white.

Born Nathan Pinchback Toomer, he lived most of his young life with his grandparents in Washington, D.C. His father left Toomer and his mother in 1895; his mother died in 1909. After graduating from Dunbar High School, one of the top black high schools in the country, he attended several universities and held a number of odd jobs before he devoted himself to writing.

Toomer began working on *Cane* in 1918. It was not written in the conventional narrative style. Instead, Toomer used stories, poems, and sketches to explore black life in Washington, D.C., and Georgia. For the Georgia sections, he drew on his observations of rural black life made during a two-month stay at Sparta Agricultural and Industrial Institute in Hancock County, Georgia, in 1921. The sections on Washington, D.C., came from his experiences in the city and from his contacts with fellow writers.

Although Harlem was generally considered the black cultural capital of the United States, scholar Kelly Miller, among others, considered Washington the Negro's heaven particularly during the 1920s. The nation's capital was home to writers and artists such as playwright Mary Burrill, poet Georgia Douglass Johnson, and scholar Alain Locke, all of whom participated in weekly gatherings at Johnson's home. Toomer is credited with the idea of these gatherings. He shared his work, as well as his philosophy of race, at these meetings.

After *Cane* was published in 1923, Toomer went to France to study with Georges I. Gurdjieff, a Russian mystic. Upon his return to the United States, Toomer led Gurdjieff workshops in Harlem and Chicago. He continued to write plays, essays, and poems on race until his death.

SELECTED PUBLICATIONS
Cane (1923)
Essentials (1931)

FURTHER READING
Benson, Brian Joseph. *Jean Toomer.* Boston:
    Twayne, 1980.
McKay, Nellie Y. *Jean Toomer, Artist: A Study
    of His Life and Work, 1894–1936.* Chapel
    Hill: University of North Carolina Press,
    1984.
Toomer, Jean. *The Collected Poems of Jean
    Toomer.* Robert B. Jones and Margery T.
    Latimer, eds. Chapel Hill: University of
    North Carolina Press, 1988.
———. *A Jean Toomer Reader: Selected
    Unpublished Writings.* New York: Oxford
    University Press, 1993.

Trotter, William Monroe

NEWSPAPER EDITOR, CIVIL RIGHTS ACTIVIST

Born: April 7, 1872
Chillicothe, Ohio

Died: April 7, 1934
Boston, Massachusetts

William Monroe Trotter, an outspoken
agitator for civil rights, was an important figure in early 20th century politics.
Trotter was uncompromising in his support
for integration, voting rights, and liberal
arts education. Through his newspaper, the
Guardian, and several protest organizations,
he was a virulent critic of racial segregation
and black leaders who suggested that African
Americans had to accommodate themselves
to segregation.

Trotter lived most of his youth in a wealthy,
predominantly white neighborhood in Boston.
He served as senior class president at his high
school and graduated with honors from
Harvard College in 1895. Trotter immersed
himself in Boston politics and in 1899 he
opened a real estate firm. Two years later he
joined a number of organizations, including
the Boston Literary and Historical Society and
the Massachusetts Racial Protective
Association (MRPA). That same year, Trotter
founded the *Guardian* newspaper with another
MRPA member, George W. Forbes. Forbes
and Trotter focused on the political and social
life of African Americans. A significant portion
of the newspaper was also devoted to attacking
those who disagreed with the views of its editors, especially members of the "Booker T.
Washington machine," as Trotter called
Washington's supporters.

Trotter was not hesitant about direct confrontation. In July 1903 Booker T. Washington
was invited to a National Negro Business
League meeting held at an African Methodist
Episcopal Zion Church in Boston. After
Washington was introduced, the audience
expressed its disapproval. While police
attempted to control the crowd, Trotter took
the opportunity to address questions to
Washington. Trotter was arrested on the
charge of conspiracy to disturb the peace and
served a month in jail. This incident became
known as the Boston Riot.

In November 1914 Trotter and other members of the National Equal Rights League met
with President Woodrow Wilson. During his
tenure in the White House, Wilson introduced
segregationist policies in federal offices, pro-
hibiting blacks and whites from sharing dining
rooms and rest rooms. Trotter condemned
Wilson for these and other policies. Offended
by Trotter's forthrightness, Wilson ended
the meeting.

In 1919, seeking to have a voice at the Paris Peace Conference following World War I, Trotter was forced to sneak into France after he was denied a passport. He wanted to ensure that the Treaty of Versailles addressed racial equality. Although unsuccessful, he was able to address the U.S. Congress upon his return.

Through his newspaper and public protests, Trotter consistently sought to influence national politics. Taking the struggle for civil rights as a mission, Trotter was a fighter throughout his life.

FURTHER READING
Fox, Stephen R. *The Guardian of Boston: William Monroe Trotter*. New York: Atheneum, 1970.

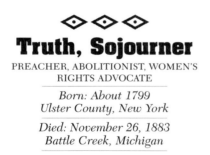

Truth, Sojourner

PREACHER, ABOLITIONIST, WOMEN'S
RIGHTS ADVOCATE

Born: About 1799
Ulster County, New York

Died: November 26, 1883
Battle Creek, Michigan

Born Isabella Bomefree in the Hudson Valley of New York State, Sojourner Truth worked for a number of white slaveowners. Her first language was Dutch. She was promised her freedom by John Dumont, for whom she worked 18 years. After he refused to carry out his promise, she escaped and was purchased by Isaac Van Wagenen, for whom she worked until she was granted freedom by state law, a year later, in 1827. (She later changed her name to Van Wagenen.) That same year, Truth experienced a religious conversion in which she felt that Jesus spoke directly to her.

Before she left Dumont's estate, Truth had married and had begun having children. After she was freed, she found out that Dumont had illegally sold one of her sons. She sued Dumont and won. She found her son in Alabama and took him back to New York, where he became a free man. Truth soon moved to New York City and began preaching.

In 1843 Isabella Bomefree changed her name to Sojourner Truth, because she felt it was her calling to seek truth. Fulfilling the meaning of her chosen identity, she left New York City and began traveling and preaching throughout the Northeast, ending up at the Northampton Association, a utopian community in Florence, Massachusetts. There she befriended abolitionists Frederick Douglass and David Ruggles and was exposed to a range of liberal thought. Truth joined the lecture circuit and began to speak out against slavery and gender oppression, becoming one of the few black women to participate in the women's rights movement.

Truth was popular on the lecture circuit in part because she was a former slave. Audiences apparently enjoyed hearing about the atrocities of enslavement from an authentic source. Truth, it seems, often embellished her life story for effect. In 1850, because she was unable to read or write, Truth dictated her life story to writer Olive Gilbert.

PUBLICATION
Narrative of Sojourner Truth (1850)

FURTHER READING
Krass, Peter. *Sojourner Truth*. New York: Chelsea House, 1988.
Painter, Nell Irwin. *Sojourner Truth: A Life, A Symbol*. New York: Norton, 1996.

Tubman, Harriet Ross

ABOLITIONIST, NURSE, ACTIVIST

Born: About 1820
Dorchester County, Maryland

Died: March 10, 1913
Auburn, New York

Before she became the best-known participant in the Underground Railroad, Harriet Tubman lived and worked for nearly 30 years as a slave on white-owned plantations in Dorchester County, Maryland. She was born Harriet Ross, probably in 1820, one of 11 children of Benjamin Ross and Harriet Green. When she was five, Harriet's master rented her to another white family to work as a domestic servant, and in her teens Harriet worked in the fields. When Tubman was 13 she was permanently injured by a blow from a white overseer, who struck her in the head with a lead weight when she attempted to protect a fleeing slave.

Tubman married a free black man, John Tubman, in 1844, but because of slave laws she remained unfree. When her master died Harriet faced the possibility of being sold to an owner in another state, so she escaped from slavery in 1849. John refused to join her, so she settled alone in Philadelphia and worked as a scrubwoman in hotels and at other jobs.

Tubman quickly involved herself in the abolitionist movement and the Underground Railroad, using the earnings from her employment to finance secret trips to the South to free enslaved blacks. After her first mission to Baltimore to retrieve her sister and her sister's children, Tubman led as many as 15 subsequent trips over the next decade, during which she helped free at least 200 black women, men, and children, including her brother's family and her parents. Tubman gained a reputation as a resourceful and tenacious rescuer. For African Americans both free and enslaved—as well as for abolitionist whites—she became an important symbol of black resistance.

Tubman worked closely with local black churches, which sheltered runaways and raised money for her trips. She also worked with prominent leaders of the abolitionist movement. In 1858 Tubman assisted John Brown in planning the raid on Harpers Ferry, Virginia.

During the Civil War, Tubman assisted the Union army, nursing injured soldiers and black refugees and spying behind enemy lines. After the war, she supported herself and her parents in Auburn, New York, by farming. She volunteered her time to help orphaned children and the elderly and to establish schools and hospitals for blacks. Tubman also continued to work extensively with black women's organizations and black churches. She served as a delegate to the 1896 meeting of the National Federation of Afro-American Women. When she died at the age of 93, Tubman was celebrated by black communities as a national hero.

FURTHER READING

Taylor, Marian. *Harriet Tubman*. New York: Chelsea House, 1991.

Turner, Nat

PREACHER, SLAVE REVOLT LEADER

Born: October 2, 1800
Southampton County, Virginia

Died: November 11, 1831
Jerusalem, Virginia

Nat Turner grew up deeply religious. His faith was influenced both by African traditions passed on to him from his family and community and by Christian values that he learned from his first master. Preaching and singing at black Baptist gatherings throughout Southampton County in the late 1820s, he became very well known among the enslaved on plantations throughout the region. In African-American churches Turner exhorted blacks to accept what his own religious convictions had taught him: that the emancipation of the enslaved was both necessary and inevitable—indeed, that it was preordained.

From an early age Turner had visions, which he interpreted as signs that he was destined to lead enslaved blacks in a revolt against their white owners. As he traveled throughout the region to preach, Turner began plans for a revolt by surveying the area and making contacts with trustworthy co-conspirators.

In 1831 a series of signs told Turner that it was time to begin. Setting out with five other slaves in late August, the insurrectionists first killed the family of Turner's master, then proceeded to other plantations in the region, gathering supporters and seizing supplies along the way. Before the local militia could suppress the uprising, perhaps as many as 80 slaves had joined the "Southampton Insurrection" and as many as 65 whites had been killed.

Those slave rebels who were not killed in battle were tried, and then either sold back into slavery or executed. After two months in hiding, Turner was finally captured. At his trial he refused to deny his actions or show remorse and was hanged on November 11, 1831.

Although the revolt was cut short, it helped destroy a popular myth—maintained by many whites at the time—that the enslaved were content with their subjugation. And because the event encouraged black slaves and many free people, both black and white, to intensify the battle for emancipation, many people refer to the rebellion as the "First War" in a decades-long battle against the institution of slavery.

FURTHER READING
Bisson, Terry. *Nat Turner.* New York: Chelsea House, 1988.
Harding, Vincent. *There Is a River: The Black Struggle for Freedom in America.* San Diego: Harcourt Brace, 1981.
Wood, Peter H. "Nat Turner: The Unknown Slave as Visionary Leader," in *Black Leaders of the Nineteenth Century,* edited by Leon Litwack and August Meier. Urbana: University of Illinois Press, 1988.

◇ ◇ ◇
Vann, Robert
JOURNALIST, PUBLISHER

Born: August 27, 1879
Ahoskie, North Carolina

Died: October 24, 1940
Pittsburgh, Pennsylvania

Robert Vann was raised in Hertford County, North Carolina, on a farm that was owned by the Albert Vann family. Robert's mother, Lucy Peoples, was employed at a neighbor's farm as a cook. At the age of 16, Robert used money he had earned from a number of jobs to enroll at the Waters Training School in Winton, North Carolina. In 1901 he began studies at Virginia Union University in Richmond, graduating in 1903. That year he started at Western University of Pennsylvania in Pittsburgh, becoming its only black student. Vann was the editor of the student paper at

Western and was selected class poet during his senior year. After graduating in 1906, he studied at Western's law school and passed the state bar in 1909.

While struggling to establish a law practice in Pittsburgh, Vann was asked in 1910 to assist with the legal incorporation and financing of a new black newsweekly, the *Pittsburgh Courier*. Established three years earlier, the *Courier* had previously focused on literature, until a group of investors set out to turn the weekly into a paper that would provide responsible news coverage of issues relevant to Pittsburgh's black residents. Vann soon took over as editor.

The *Courier's* new format was very popular with African Americans living in Pittsburgh, because the paper covered news in the black community and because Vann used his editorials to speak out about current political issues that white papers would not discuss. In its pages, Vann supported civil rights reforms, promoted black entrepreneurship, and made demands on the city government to improve living and working conditions for the city's black residents.

In order to expand circulation and attract a national readership, Vann gradually shifted the paper's focus and devoted more space to issues that would interest blacks throughout the United States. Along with the Chicago *Defender,* the *Courier* eventually helped define political issues for a national black readership and often proposed tactics for the fight against Jim Crow discrimination. The *Courier* provided in-depth coverage of the war between Italy and Ethiopia and carefully reported the struggles of A. Philip Randolph and the Brotherhood of Sleeping Car Porters. The

Courier's coverage of Joe Louis's career helped make the boxer an important national symbol of black struggle and survival.

By the 1930s, the *Courier* had the largest format of any African-American newspaper in the country, and its circulation was expanding rapidly. After Vann died of cancer in 1940, the paper continued to cover and support black political struggles, reaching its peak circulation of 357,000 in 1947. Readership declined sharply in the 1950s and 1960s, as African Americans increasingly turned to other sources for national news.

FURTHER READING
Buni, Andrew. *Robert L. Vann and the Pittsburgh Courier: Politics and Black Journalism.* Pittsburgh: University of Pittsburgh Press, 1974.
Ingham, John N., and Lynne B. Feldman, eds. *African American Business Leaders: A Biographical Dictionary*. Westport, Conn.: Greenwood, 1994.

Van Peebles, Melvin
FILMMAKER, ACTOR, PLAYWRIGHT

Born: August 21, 1932
Chicago, Illinois

With his third film, *Sweet Sweetback's Baadasssss Song* (1971), Melvin Van Peebles ushered in a new wave of black films popularly known as blaxploitation. These action-packed films introduced a sexual and aggressive black male (but sometimes female) character on movie screens throughout the country. Although Van Peebles is most known for *Sweet Sweetback,* he has also authored five novels, written and produced plays, and acted in film and theater.

Van Peebles lived most of his youth in a Chicago suburb. He attended Ohio Wesleyan University, where he received a degree in literature in 1953. After college he served a brief stint in the U.S. Air Force.

Van Peebles began making films in California, but he decided to move to Europe to launch his career. In France, he began writing novels and made his first film, *Story of a Three-Day Pass* (1967), about interracial love. The success of *Three-Day Pass* landed him a contract with Columbia Pictures to make *Watermelon Man,* featuring actor Godfrey Cambridge, about a white man who turned black.

As he recounts in his book *The Making of Sweet Sweetback's Baadasssss Song* (1971), Van Peebles decided that he needed to control all aspects of it—writing, directing, producing, and financing. By March 1970 Van Peebles had written the screenplay. He shot the film in only 19 days. The movie opened at the Grand Circus Theatre in Detroit, Michigan, on March 31, 1971, and was an instant hit.

Van Peebles's contemporaries include Ossie Davis, Gordon Parks, Sr., and Gordon Parks, Jr.; the latter two made *Shaft* (1971) and *Superfly* (1972), respectively. Both films capitalized on the success of *Sweet Sweetback* by using the black superhero theme. In the 1970s, black actors, writers, and directors were used more than they had ever been. In addition, Hollywood recognized African-American moviegoers as an important market and began to produce films with them in mind.

Van Peebles produced a Broadway musical, *Ain't Supposed to Die a Natural Death,* in 1972. That same year, he directed *Don't Play*

Us Cheap, based on his novel *A Harlem Party*. In 1973 he went on tour with his one-man show *Out There by Your Lonesome*.

After working on Wall Street as a trader, Van Peebles wrote two how-to books on options trading. More recently, he has collaborated with his actor-director son, Mario Van Peebles, on films.

FILMS
The Story of a Three-Day Pass (1967)
Watermelon Man (1969)
Sweet Sweetback's Baadasssss Song (1971)
Don't Play Us Cheap (1973)
Identity Crisis (1989, with son Mario Van Peebles)

PUBLICATIONS
The Making of Sweet Sweetback's Baadasssss Song (1971)
Just an Old Sweet Song (1976)

FURTHER READING
Bogle, Donald. *Toms, Coons, Mulattoes, Mammies, and Bucks: An Interpretive History of Blacks in American Films*. New York: Continuum, 1993.
Cripps, Thomas. *Making Movies Black: The Hollywood Message Movie from World War II to the Civil Rights Era*. New York: Oxford University Press, 1993.

Vesey, Denmark
SLAVE REBELLION LEADER

Born: about 1767
Probably in Africa

Died: July 2, 1822
Charleston, South Carolina

Denmark Vesey—a name that he would not adopt until his teens—was born in Africa, or perhaps in the Caribbean, probably in 1767. In 1781 he was sold to a slave trader in St. Thomas, Virgin Islands. Denmark was enslaved next on a plantation in St. Dominique, then in Bermuda, and then on board the ship of a slave trader, Joseph Vesey, before settling with his new master in Charleston, South Carolina. In 1799, at the age of 33, Denmark Vesey won enough money in a lottery to purchase his freedom. Vesey was self-educated and fluent in several languages. He opened a woodworking shop in Charleston and began to contribute to the struggle against slavery.

In 1821, Vesey began to plan and organize for an armed assault on Charleston. He recruited enslaved artisans from throughout the region, many of whom he had met during his years of work as a carpenter. The conspirators met at Vesey's carpentry shop and in a local black church, where they read abolitionist pamphlets, discussed current events (such as white authorities' suppression of local black churches), and debated revolutionary ideas. Vesey and his co-conspirators were especially interested in the legacy of the French and American revolutions, and the successful revolt by the enslaved blacks of St. Dominique (Haiti). The conspirators also found ideas and inspiration for their struggles in the Bible.

By the spring of 1822, Vesey and the others had formulated a plan to capture the arsenal and guardhouse in Charleston, to start a series of fires, and then to kill whites who were trying to flee their homes. But one of the blacks that Vesey tried to recruit told his owner about their plans. The plot unraveled as white authorities arrested the participants, executing 37 and deporting another 43. Vesey and his closest allies were hanged on July 2.

South Carolina officials and slaveowners reacted to Vesey's rebellion by passing legislation that even further restricted the movement of both enslaved and free blacks. The Vesey rebellion was one of several slave revolts during these years that led many Southern states to pass similar legislation. This intensified the debate between slave states and the federal government over the South's right to defend the institution of slavery.

FURTHER READING

Aptheker, Herbert. *American Negro Slave Revolts*. 5th ed. New York: International, 1983.

Edwards, Lillie J. *Denmark Vesey*. New York: Chelsea House, 1990.

Lofton, John. *Denmark Vesey's Revolt: The Slave Plot That Lit a Fuse to Fort Sumter*. Kent, Ohio: Kent State University Press, 1983.

Walker, David

ABOLITIONIST, PUBLICIST

Born: 1785
Wilmington, North Carolina

Died: June 28, 1830
Boston, Massachusetts

Because his mother was free, Walker was born legally free even though his father was enslaved. After receiving an informal education, he spent much of his life traveling through the American South and West, observing the working and living conditions of enslaved blacks. In 1826, at the age of 41, he settled in Boston, where he established a clothing shop and quickly set out to support the black community and to popularize abolitionist ideas.

His Boston home became a place of refuge for free blacks and fugitive slaves. Walker was an organizer and lecturer for a black abolitionist organization, the General Colored Association of Massachusetts. He wrote for the abolitionist publication *Rights for All* and was the Boston agent for America's first black newspaper, *Freedom's Journal,* which encouraged free blacks to use the vote to destroy slavery.

By 1828, Walker used his lectures to encourage measures far more radical than those found in the pages of antislavery journals of the time. The following year, he published *Walker's Appeal . . . to the Colored Citizens of the World, But in Particular and very Expressly to those of the United States of America,* which marked the first time that a black man directly attacked slavery in an American publication. Walker argued that slavery degraded all people of African descent, both enslaved and free. In an acute analysis of the institution of slavery, he explained that white racism was firmly rooted in the economic exploitation of unfree black labor. Walker insisted that in order to destroy slavery, free blacks must support the enslaved, and African Americans must demonstrate their solidarity with people of African descent throughout the world. Since whites would certainly resist black organization and protest, Walker wrote, blacks should prepare themselves for armed struggle.

Walker was a devout Methodist, and his faith in God informed his critique of American racism, his appeal for solidarity, and his advocacy of struggle. Writing that slavery defied God's will and natural law, Walker predicted that God would seek retribution against whites

for their sins against Africans and against humanity.

White Southerners immediately suppressed the distribution of the *Appeal*. Even Northern white abolitionists attacked Walker's writings, despite his appeals to religious faith and to human rights and dignity. Walker predicted in the *Appeal* that he would likely be killed for advocating such radical views. On June 28, 1830, less than a year after publication of the *Appeal*, Walker suddenly collapsed and died at his Boston clothing store, probably the victim of a poisoning.

Walker's writings and deeds set a powerful precedent for a generation of abolitionist writing and activism. The *Appeal* continued to circulate widely among free and enslaved blacks long after Walker's death.

PUBLICATION
Walker's Appeal . . . to the Colored Citizens of the World, But in Particular and very Expressly to those of the United States of America (1829)

FURTHER READING
Harding, Vincent. *There Is a River: The Black Struggle for Freedom in America.* San Diego: Harcourt Brace, 1981.

◇ ◇ ◇
Walker, Madam C. J.
ENTREPRENEUR, PHILANTHROPIST

Born: December 23, 1867
near Delta, Louisiana

Died: May 12, 1919
Irvington-on-Hudson, New York

Madam C. J. Walker was born Sarah Breedlove, the daughter of former slaves and sharecroppers Owen and Minerva Breedlove. Breedlove's parents died when she was seven years old, so she moved to Vicksburg, Mississippi, to live with her sister. In order to escape the abuse of her sister's husband, Sarah married at age 14. She soon had a daughter, Lelia (who later changed her name to A'Lelia). After Sarah's husband was killed in 1887, she moved to St. Louis, where for 18 years she supported herself and her daughter by working as a washerwoman.

During this time, she began to experiment with hair treatments in order to curb her own hair loss. After working as an agent for Annie M. Malone, a pioneer of black cosmetic products, Breedlove eventually perfected a series of hair and skin treatments. She moved to Denver in 1906 and began to market her products door-to-door. That year she married Charles Joseph Walker, a newspaper sales agent. With the help of her sister-in-law, her nieces, her daughter, and Charles, Sarah Walker (now known as Madam C. J. Walker) established a huge market for her line of hair and cosmetic products. She trained agents to demonstrate the "Walker System," which eventually included "Wonderful Hair Grower," "Glossine" hair oil, and a redesigned steel hot comb specifically suited for black women's hair. The Madam C. J. Walker Manufacturing Company—which included a mail-order operation and two beauty schools—quickly became one of the most profitable independently owned businesses in the country.

Walker traveled throughout the United States and Caribbean to promote her products, which she saw both as a way to make hair care and hygiene more convenient for black women

and as a means to promote black business. Critics accused her of encouraging black women to aspire to "European" standards of female beauty. But the Walker method became enormously popular, eventually influencing black hair styles throughout the United States, the West Indies, and as far away as France.

Madam Walker took great pride in enabling black women to achieve economic independence and in encouraging them to balance their work and family lives. Her company created new careers for as many as 25,000 black women—as salespeople and "demonstrators" of Walker products, as beauticians in the parlors that Madam Walker established in the United States and abroad, and as factory workers in the Walker plant. The "Walker Agents," who wore white blouses and long black skirts when promoting the Walker techniques, became common sights in black communities and were symbols of black business savvy and economic independence.

The company made Madam Walker a millionaire. She used part of her fortune to support black institutions and organizations, including the NAACP and homes for the elderly. She sponsored scholarships for black women and helped fund black schools, including Mary McLeod Bethune's Daytona Educational and Industrial Institute in Florida. She was an active supporter of anti-lynching campaigns and an outspoken critic of European colonialism after World War I.

FURTHER READING
Bundles, A'Lelia Perry. *Madam C. J. Walker*. New York: Chelsea House, 1991.

Walker, Maggie Lena Mitchell

BUSINESSWOMAN

Born: July 15, 1867
Richmond, Virginia

Died: December 15, 1934
Richmond, Virginia

Maggie Lena Walker helped to create a thriving economic institution in Richmond, Virginia, that, under her leadership, was replicated in over 20 states. Walker lived most of her life in Richmond and attended Armstrong Normal School there. Her high school class was noted for its protest against segregation. White seniors had their graduation ceremonies in the Richmond Theater; black seniors were forced to use a local church. Walker and her nine classmates demanded use of the theater. Although they were unsuccessful, their activism was publicized nationally. After graduation in 1883, Walker taught for three years. She had to quit teaching after she married, because only single women were allowed to be teachers.

Walker became involved in the Independent Order of St. Luke (IOSL), a mutual aid society founded in 1867, while she was in high school. She became part of the leadership in 1899, creating a Juvenile Department and a Council of Matrons, which ensured that women and men were partners in the development of the IOSL. As executive secretary and treasurer, she helped transform the fledgling organization into a financially solvent enterprise. Her success enabled her to lead the IOSL for more than 30 years. Walker expanded the original aims of the organization by founding a bank, newspaper, hotel, and grocery store. Through these enterprises, she provided needed jobs and skills to women and men in Richmond.

In turn-of-the-century Richmond, African Americans' civil rights were being slowly eroded. Increased voting restrictions and segregation in housing and employment propelled African Americans toward a philosophy of self-help and institution building. The Grand Fountain United Order of True Reformers, another fraternal organization, founded the first black bank in Richmond in 1888. The St. Luke Penny Savings Bank, which Walker opened in 1903, continues today as the Consolidated Bank and Trust Company.

In 1912 Walker founded the Council of Colored Women. She was also a member of the National Association of Colored Women, National Association for the Advancement of Colored People, and the National Urban League.

During the last six years of her life, Walker relied on the use of a wheelchair. She had an elevator installed in her house and had her car made wheelchair accessible, which enabled her to get around as needed.

FURTHER READING

Brown, Elsa Barkley. "Womanist Consciousness: Maggie Lena Walker and the Independent Order of St. Luke." *Signs*, Spring 1989.

Washington, Booker Taliaferro

EDUCATOR, COMMUNITY LEADER

Born: About 1856
near Hale's Ford, Virginia

Died: November 14, 1915
Tuskegee, Alabama

Booker T. Washington was a complex leader who carefully constructed a public and private persona. In public, particularly to whites, he was an accommodationist, one who accepted the limited rights of African Americans. In private, Washington was a political activist, who financed numerous desegregation court cases. As founder and president of Tuskegee Institute, founder of the National Negro Business League, and owner of several black newspapers, Washington was able to amass a strong power base, the "Tuskegee Machine," that was respected and feared by both blacks and whites.

Washington was born enslaved in Virginia. His mother was black and his father, whom he never knew, was white. As a child he worked mostly as a houseboy. After emancipation he moved with his mother to West Virginia, where he continued to work as a house servant for a wealthy white man. Washington attended Hampton Institute in Hampton, Virginia. He paid for his schooling by working around the school. His experience at Hampton impressed on him the importance of hard work and sacrifice.

In 1881, six years after leaving Hampton, Washington founded his own school, Tuskegee Normal and Industrial Institute. At Tuskegee, Washington emphasized industrial education—training in agricultural production and other skills such as cooking and carpentry that would enable African Americans to build an economic base. This philosophy fit well with whites who wanted African Americans to continue to work as sharecroppers on plantations and farms as they had before emancipation. The school was largely financed by white philanthropists and businessmen. Washington's emphasis on self-empowerment also encouraged blacks to open their own businesses,

which led to the development of banks, printing shops, florists, and department stores.

In 1895, at the Cotton States and International Exposition in Atlanta, Washington expounded on his accommodationist philosophy in a speech that is commonly called the Atlanta Compromise. Washington stressed social separation of blacks and whites. Further, he believed that blacks could only advance and gain respect from whites through hard work and economic self-sufficiency.

Washington's leadership was opposed by Ida B. Wells-Barnett, W. E. B. Du Bois, and William Monroe Trotter, among others. These three leaders were tenacious, public fighters of segregation who felt that African Americans could not afford to wait for whites to treat them as full citizens.

Much of Washington's philosophy can be found in his autobiography, *Up from Slavery* (1901), which details his rise to prominence.

PUBLICATIONS
Up from Slavery (1901, reprint 1995)
The Negro in Business (1907)

FURTHER READING
Harlan, Louis R. *Booker T. Washington: The Making of a Black Leader, 1856–1901.* New York: Oxford University Press, 1983.
Schroeder, Alan. *Booker T. Washington.* New York: Chelsea House, 1992.

◇ ◇ ◇
Washington, Harold
POLITICIAN

Born: April 15, 1922
Chicago, Illinois

Died: November 25, 1987
Chicago, Illinois

Harold Washington was raised in Chicago by his father, Ray Lee Washington, after the elder Washington separated from Harold's mother, Bertha. Ray Lee, an African Methodist Episcopal minister, worked in the Chicago stockyards, earned a law degree by taking night classes, and served as a Democratic precinct captain in the city's third ward. Harold had some of his first lessons in politics during conversations with his father at the dinner table.

Washington dropped out of high school after the 11th grade, then earned his high school equivalency certificate while serving in the U.S. Army during World War II. In 1949, Washington earned a degree in political science from Roosevelt University in Chicago. Three years later he was the only black in the graduating class of Northwestern University's law school.

After Ray Lee Washington's death in 1953, Harold took over his father's job as ward precinct captain and proved himself a very capable organizer. During this time he also participated in numerous independent black political organizations and served as assistant prosecutor for the city of Chicago.

Beginning in the mid-1960s, Washington successfully ran for state and city offices by taking an independent path from the established Democratic party organization, or "machine." From 1965 to 1980 he served in the Illinois state legislature, all the while maintaining links to independent black political organizations. He attracted a loyal constituency by courageously fighting for the rights of the elderly, women, and working people. In 1977 he made an unsuccessful bid for mayor of Chicago.

Three years later Washington was elected to the U.S. House of Representatives, where he was a vocal spokesman for the rights of minorities, and a strong critic of the Reagan administration's emphasis on defense spending. Back in Chicago, many black people who were frustrated with the local Democratic party had been organizing alternative bases for political power. After grassroots coalitions mounted a massive voter registration drive and an extensive fundraising campaign in Chicago's black wards, Washington agreed to run for mayor again in 1983. He won 51.5 percent of the vote, becoming the first black mayor of the city.

Washington implemented affirmative action policies designed to help women and members of minority groups obtain city jobs and municipal contracts. He tried to clean up hiring and campaign finance practices, helped finance the improvement of city-run facilities, and worked to revive the city's retail and manufacturing sectors. Throughout his time in office, however, Washington's most controversial initiatives were repeatedly struck down by a hostile Democratic city council. Soon after his election to a second term in 1987, Washington died of a heart attack, cutting short his administration's experiment with municipal reform.

FURTHER READING
Kleppner, Paul. *Chicago Divided: The Making of a Black Mayor*. De Kalb: Northern Illinois University Press, 1985.

Weaver, Robert Clifton
GOVERNMENT OFFICIAL, SCHOLAR

Born: December 29, 1907
Washington, D.C.

Weaver was raised in a mostly white, middle-class neighborhood in the District of Columbia by his mother, Florence Freeman, and his father, Mortimer Grover Weaver. After attending primary and secondary schools in Washington, he went on to graduate from Harvard University in 1929 and earn master's and doctorate degrees in economics there. In 1933 he accepted a position as an adviser on race relations for the Housing Division of the U.S. Department of the Interior. Weaver became an important voice in the so-called Black Cabinet during President Franklin D. Roosevelt's administration.

After leaving the Housing Division in 1938, Weaver worked in a number of advisory and policy positions for the U.S. government, for the city of Chicago, for the state of New York, and for private coalitions and foundations. In all of these positions Weaver focused on making housing, employment, and educational resources available to African Americans. He published several important studies of black employment and housing conditions, including *The Negro Ghetto* (1948) and *Dilemmas of Urban America* (1965).

In recognition of his work, President Kennedy appointed Weaver director of the U.S. Housing and Home Finance Agency in 1961. In 1965, President Johnson selected Weaver to run the newly created Department of Housing and Urban Development. In his work with these agencies, Weaver initiated a number of innovative programs designed to make quality housing available to poor families, the ill, and the elderly. He also proposed plans to help end the illegal segregation of neighborhoods and to secure government aid for impoverished urban areas. Many of Weaver's initiatives were blocked by hostile

white elected officials or had only a limited impact because the government refused to fund them adequately.

Weaver retired from the government in 1969 to serve as president of Baruch College in New York City. From 1971 until 1978, he taught urban affairs at New York's Hunter College. From 1973 until 1987 he served as president of the National Committee Against Discrimination in Housing. He has also worked with groups including the American Jewish Congress and the Citizens' Committee for Children. He lives in New York City.

SELECTED PUBLICATIONS
Negro Labor: A National Problem (1946)
Dilemmas of Urban America (1965)

FURTHER READING
Kirby, John B. *Black Americans in the Roosevelt Era: Liberalism and Race.* Knoxville: University of Tennessee Press, 1980.
Sitkoff, Harvard. *A New Deal for Blacks: The Emergence of Civil Rights as a National Issue.* New York: Oxford University Press, 1978.

Wells-Barnett, Ida Bell

JOURNALIST, ACTIVIST

*Born: July 16, 1862
Holly Springs, Mississippi*

*Died: March 25, 1931
Chicago, Illinois*

Ida B. Wells was born into slavery in 1862, one of eight children of Jim Wells, a carpenter, and Elizabeth Warrenton, a cook. After emancipation, her parents became involved in Reconstruction politics and supported local efforts to establish Shaw University (later Rust

College) in Holly Springs. Ida attended the grammar school at Shaw, but was left with much of the responsibility for taking care of her family when her parents died in 1878. Ida helped support her siblings by teaching school, first in Holly Springs, then in rural Tennessee, and finally in Memphis from 1884 to 1891.

During her years in Memphis, Wells participated in weekly meetings held by local high school teachers. In addition to playing music and discussing essays, the group read from the *Evening Star,* a journal of current events that circulated only among members of the group. When Wells took over the editorship of this paper, her work gained her the attention of the black community, and a local Baptist church asked her to contribute a column to its weekly paper. Wells was soon writing columns for a number of Southern Baptist papers, using the pen name "Iola." In 1889 she was elected secretary of the newly created Colored Press Association (later the Afro-American Press Association), and was invited to edit the *Free Speech and Headlight,* an outspoken black Baptist paper in Memphis.

From the beginning of her career as a journalist, Wells focused on civil rights issues and black political struggles. Some of her first contributions to the Baptist papers detailed her experiences fighting Jim Crow laws, including her 1884 lawsuit against a railroad company that removed her from a train when she refused to leave the first-class compartment. Wells's outspoken editorials aroused much controversy, as she proposed increasingly militant responses to white violence. The Memphis school board fired Wells after she published an article critical of the system's lack of support for African-American education. After three of her friends were lynched by a white mob in 1892, Wells used *Free Speech* to support a boycott of the local streetcar line and the exodus of 2,000 blacks from the city.

In May of that year, while Wells was attending a convention in Philadelphia, she published an editorial in *Free Speech* that directly challenged the myth that black men were being lynched for raping white women. Outraged by the essay, the local white press immediately called for the murder of Wells. On the night of the 27th, the offices of *Free Speech* were destroyed. Wells did not return to Memphis.

She continued her campaign against lynching by writing a series of columns for the *New York Age* (which distributed its papers to former *Free Speech* subscribers). After adding new material, Wells republished the series in two booklets that were circulated throughout the country: *Southern Horrors* (1892) and *A Red Record: Tabulated Statistics and Alleged Causes of Lynching in the United States* (1895). Wells lectured in Northern and Western states and in Great Britain and organized local anti-lynching societies. Her writings, lectures, and highly publicized exile from the South brought both the writer and the anti-lynching campaign enormous national and international publicity. Although the campaign was met by hostility from most whites and hesitance from many blacks, Wells fought tirelessly for federal anti-lynching legislation throughout her life.

Wells settled in Chicago in the mid-1890s, married Ferdinand L. Barnett, and had four children. Though her familial obligations kept her from traveling as extensively as she had in the past, she continued to write on lynching, race riots, and other issues. And she participated in dozens of political campaigns and organizations that sought to protect the physical safety of black Americans and their rights to housing and employment. Wells-Barnett participated in the founding of the National Association of Colored Women in 1896, and in 1910 founded the Negro Fellowship League in Chicago, which helped male migrants find housing and jobs.

She was a member of the first executive committee of the National Association for the Advancement of Colored People (NAACP)—although her relationships with its founding members were strained—and she later supported Marcus Garvey's Universal Negro Improvement Association (UNIA). In 1930 she ran unsuccessfully for the U.S. Senate. When she died the following year at the age of 68, Wells-Barnett had long grown estranged from many of the movements to which she had contributed throughout her life. Nonetheless, her efforts as a journalist, spokesperson, and organizer had been crucial to sustaining radical political protest by African Americans for decades, and they helped set the stage for civil rights activities that would follow.

SELECTED PUBLICATIONS
Crusade for Justice (autobiography, published posthumously in 1970)
On Lynchings (1900, reprinted 1969)

FURTHER READING
DeCosta-Willis, Miriam, ed. *The Memphis Diary of Ida B. Wells.* Boston: Beacon, 1995.
Holt, Thomas C. "The Lonely Warrior: Ida B. Wells-Barnett and the Struggle for Black Leadership," in John Hope Franklin and August Meier, eds. *Black Leaders of the Twentieth Century.* Urbana: University of Illinois Press, 1992.

Van Steenwyck, Elizabeth. *Ida B. Wells-Barnett: Woman of Courage.* New York: Watts, 1992.

Wheatley, Phillis
POET

Born: About 1753
Gambia, West Africa

Died: December 5, 1784
Boston, Massachusetts

Phillis Wheatley was one of millions of Africans captured by white slavers and brought to North America to be enslaved. She was renamed by the Wheatleys, white Bostonians who purchased her after her voyage on the ship *Phillis*.

Wheatley was taught to read and write by the Wheatleys' children. She proved an able student, learning to read and write in about 16 months. By the following year she was able to read Latin. Particularly fond of the Bible and the Greek poet Homer, Wheatley read and studied a range of subjects and began writing poetry when she was 12. Apparently her owners indulged her talents; while serving as Ms. Wheatley's servant she was allowed to pursue her poetry.

Boston, the literary capital of the United States at that time, was also home to a small black community. Blacks had been there since 1638, when enslaved Africans were brought there to be sold. Other blacks in Boston in the late 18th century were artist Scipio Moorehead and writer Briton Hammon. Briton Hammon and Jupiter Hammon were the first blacks to publish their writings. Wheatley is usually credited with this distinction, but the Hammons had a pamphlet and poem, respectively, published in 1760. Wheatley was probably, however, the first to publish a book.

Wheatley's first book, *Poems on Various Subjects, Religious and Moral* (1773), was published in London. None of the white publishing companies in Boston would publish it. The same year that her book was issued, she gained her freedom. The themes of Wheatley's poetry focused on her life in Boston and her observations of other Bostonians. Though she rarely addressed the issue of slavery or race in her poetry, her antislavery statements appeared in newspapers. Phillis Wheatley died as a result of childbirth complications at the age of 31.

PUBLICATIONS
Poems on Various Subjects, Religious and Moral (1773)
The Collected Works of Phillis Wheatley (John C. Shields, ed., 1988)

FURTHER READING
Richmond, Merle A. *Phillis Wheatley*. New York: Chelsea House, 1988.
Rinaldi, Ann. *Hang a Thousand Trees with Ribbons: The Story of Phillis Wheatley*. San Diego: Harcourt Brace, 1996.

White, Walter Francis
CIVIL RIGHTS ACTIVIST, AUTHOR

Born: July 1, 1893
Atlanta, Georgia

Died: March 21, 1955
New York, New York

Walter White was raised in a middle-class home in Atlanta. When White was 13, a race riot broke out in Atlanta that would teach him a great deal about his racial identity. White was very fair skinned, with blue eyes and blond hair. He could easily "pass" for white. Yet on the day of the riot he found himself clutching a gun in a darkened room of his home as he and his father prepared to fight off a mob of violent whites. This episode, White would explain years later, helped him to understand clearly that he would not be comfortable hiding behind his "white" appearance. It was also one of the episodes that convinced him to commit his life to struggle for the rights and safety of all African Americans.

Attending Atlanta University, White played football and participated on the debate team while working part time for a life insurance company. After graduation in 1916, he continued his work in insurance full time. He also helped organize a new chapter of the NAACP in Atlanta and helped campaign against the local school board's attempt to eliminate seventh-grade education for the city's blacks. White's work in the successful campaign attracted the attention of James Weldon Johnson—then head of the NAACP— who invited him to New York City to work at the organization's headquarters.

In 1918, White accepted an office job at the NAACP, yet soon focused his efforts on investigating the lynching of blacks. Between World War I and World War II, White used his ability to "pass" as white to investigate forty-two lynchings and eight race riots. White published his initial findings in 1929, in an effort to gather support for anti-lynching legislation and other civil rights reforms.

White officially succeeded Johnson as secretary of the NAACP in 1931 and led the organization until 1955. During White's tenure, the NAACP continued to broaden its strategies for dismantling segregation and discrimination, and became a major lobbying force that held considerable political weight in Washington, D.C. Under White's leadership, the NAACP worked to protect blacks from white racist violence, to secure blacks' voting rights, to outlaw residential segregation, and to end discrimination in higher education, the armed forces, and civilian employment. When the U.S. Senate refused White's request to investigate racism in the armed forces, he convinced the NAACP to support A. Philip Randolph's "March on Washington" campaign in 1941.

White was also an influential author and an important contributor to the Harlem Renaissance. He wrote novels, essays for a number of national periodicals, and weekly columns for black and white newspapers. Along with James Weldon Johnson, Jessie Fauset, W. E. B. Du Bois, and others, White helped introduced the work of young black novelists and poets to publishers and to readers.

SELECTED PUBLICATIONS
Fire in the Flint (1924, reprint 1969)
Flight (1926)
A Man Called White (1948, reprint 1969)

FURTHER READING
Sitkoff, Harvard. *A New Deal for Blacks: The Emergence of Civil Rights as a National Issue.* New York: Oxford University Press, 1978.
Waldron, Edward E. *Walter White and the Harlem Renaissance.* Port Washington, N.Y.: Kennikat Press, 1978.

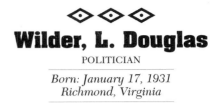

Wilder, L. Douglas
POLITICIAN

Born: January 17, 1931
Richmond, Virginia

Douglas Wilder was born in the black neighborhood of Church Hill, the child of Beulah and Robert Wilder. Douglas worked at a variety of jobs while attending Armstrong High School and later to pay his tuition at Virginia Union University, where he studied chemistry. After he graduated in 1952, Wilder was drafted into the U.S. Army to serve in Korea, where he lived and worked in an integrated environment for the first time.

Upon returning to civilian life, Wilder was unable to find work as a chemist; white employers recommended that he take unskilled jobs instead. Outraged by white racism, and inspired by the 1954 Supreme Court decision in *Brown* v. *Board of Education,* he decided to attend law school. After graduating from Howard University's law school, he opened a practice in 1959 in the neighborhood where he had grown up. Wilder established a reputation as a skilled criminal defense attorney and grew quite wealthy by taking on personal injury cases.

In 1969 he became the first African American to win a seat in Virginia's state senate. Wilder had not been active in black protest politics before his election, and he did not focus on civil rights issues during his years in the senate. Indeed, as Wilder's influence grew over the course of his 16 years in office, he became increasingly conservative in many policy areas that affected black people. Yet because Wilder had been an outspoken critic of white politicians' racist slogans and policies, some came to see him as a spokesperson for blacks in the state.

In 1985 Wilder won the race for lieutenant governor, becoming the first African American ever elected to statewide office in Virginia. In 1989 he became the Democratic party's nominee for governor and won the general election, again a first for an African American. While in office, he attracted a great deal of criticism, especially from liberals upset by his leadership style and his support for the death penalty. Since leaving office, Wilder has hosted a radio talk show in Virginia and lectured around the country.

FURTHER READING
Edds, Margaret. *Claiming the Dream: The Victorious Campaign of Douglas Wilder of Virginia*. Chapel Hill, N.C.: Algonquin, 1990.

Woodson, Carter Godwin
HISTORIAN

Born: December 19, 1875
New Canton, Virginia

Died: April 3, 1950
Washington, D.C.

Carter G. Woodson, known as the "Father of Negro History," helped create the basis for today's vital African-American studies. Part of the first generation of academically trained historians, he was committed to advancing the field of African-American history (as well as U.S. and world history) in the university, secondary schools, and among the general public.

Woodson grew up in Buckingham County, Virginia. After the Civil War, his parents worked as sharecroppers until they were able to purchase their own land. Woodson worked on the family farm and as an agricultural day laborer. In the late 1880s his family moved to West Virginia, where Woodson worked as a coal miner. In 1895, at the age of 20, he started high school. Woodson graduated in two years. He graduated from Berea College in Kentucky in 1903 and spent the next four years as a teacher in the Philippines.

Upon his return to the United States, Woodson continued his education at the University of Chicago. He earned a B.A. (1907) and an M.A. (1908) in European history. In 1912 he received his Ph.D. in history from Harvard University. Woodson then moved to Washington, D.C., and found work as a teacher and administrator in the public school system and at Howard University. In September 1915 he founded the Association for the Study of Negro Life and History. Four months later, the first issue of the *Journal of Negro History* was completed. To promote the publication and dissemination of black history, Woodson established Associated Publishers in 1920. In February 1926, he launched Negro History Week, and he chose February as Negro History Month because it was the month of Frederick Douglass's and Abraham Lincoln's birth. Woodson also founded the *Negro History Bulletin* in 1937 to encourage the study and understanding of black history among a lay audience.

SELECTED PUBLICATIONS
Free Negro Heads of Families in the United States in 1830 (1925)

The Miseducation of the Negro (1933)
The African Background Outlined (1936)
African Heroes and Heroines (1939)

FURTHER READING

Goggin, Jacqueline Anne. *Carter G. Woodson: A Life in Black History.* Baton Rouge: Louisiana State University Press, 1993.

Greene, Lorenzo Johnston. *Working with Carter G. Woodson, the Father of Black History: A Diary, 1928–1930.* Baton Rouge: Louisiana State University Press, 1989.

Scally, M. A. *Walking Proud: The Story of Dr. Carter Godwin Woodson.* Washington, D.C.: Associated Publishers, 1983.

Work, Monroe Nathan

BIBLIOGRAPHER, SOCIOLOGIST

Born: August 15, 1866
Tredell County, North Carolina

Died: May 2, 1945
Tuskegee, Alabama

Monroe Work's life was devoted to collecting data and writing about African Americans. Work, like historian Carter G. Woodson and library builders Arthur Alphonso Schomburg and Dorothy Porter Wesley, believed that statistics and other data were important to an understanding of the experience of African Americans. Work's publications and statistical analyses have been instrumental in the development of the field of African-American studies as well as the black health movement and anti-lynching efforts.

Work was born in rural North Carolina to formerly enslaved parents. The family, which included 11 brothers and sisters, migrated westward to Cairo, Illinois, and then to Kansas, where they bought a farm. Work's schooling was intermittent; he did not begin high school until he was 23; he graduated in 1892, at 26.

After graduation, Work pursued a career in the church. He became a pastor of an African Methodist Episcopal church and graduated from the Chicago Theological Seminary in 1898. He decided to continue his education at the University of Chicago; he earned a B.A. in 1902 and a master's degree the following year. Work then left for Savannah, Georgia, to teach at Georgia State Industrial College.

After four years at Georgia State, Work accepted Booker T. Washington's offer to head Tuskegee Institute's Department of Records and Research. In this position, he collected written materials and data on African Americans, which led to the publication of the *Negro Yearbook, Annual Encyclopedia of the Negro.* The *Yearbook,* which Work edited from 1912 to 1938, provided a compendium of facts about black life in the United States, the Caribbean, Europe, and Africa. In 1927 Work completed *A Bibliography of the Negro in Africa and America,* a monumental effort that listed books, articles, and pamphlets by and about blacks in Africa and the United States.

Before taking the position at Tuskegee, Work founded the Savannah Men's Sunday Club, a civic club and protest organization in 1905. He was inspired by a 1905 conference called by W. E. B. Du Bois that led to the development of the Niagara Movement and later the National Association for the Advancement of Colored People. In 1914 Work's statistical analyses of the health of Southern blacks, which found that nearly half of all black deaths could have been prevented, were used by local health activists to start National Negro Health Week. Work also directed the annual compilation of Tuskegee Lynching Records.

PUBLICATION
A Bibliography of the Negro in Africa and America (1927)

FURTHER READING
McMurry, Linda O. *Recorder of the Black Experience: A Biography of Monroe Nathan Work*. Baton Rouge: Louisiana State University Press, 1985.

Wright, Richard
NOVELIST

*Born: September 4, 1908
near Roxie, Mississippi*

*Died: November 28, 1960
Paris, France*

Richard Wright set the standards by which later African-American writers would be judged. He grew up in poverty and, because of his mother's ill health, was shuttled between various family members in Mississippi and Tennessee. He began writing at a young age and had his first story published in a local newspaper in 1925. As soon as he was able, he migrated to Chicago.

There Wright worked as a postal clerk. In his spare time, he continued to work on his craft. In 1932 Wright joined a group of writers and artists, many of whom were communists; soon he was contributing articles to leftist publications. Three years later, Wright found work with the Federal Writers Project and the Federal Theater Project of the Works Project Administration.

Wright moved to New York in 1937 and became the Harlem reporter for *The Daily Worker,* a communist newspaper. His first published book, *Uncle Tom's Children* (1938), was a collection of short stories; many of these won prizes. It is the novel *Native Son* (1940), however, that established Wright as a formidable writer.

Native Son introduces protagonist Bigger Thomas, a member of the Chicago working class, who is so overwhelmed by racism that he commits murder. Ironically, it is through murder that Bigger Thomas discovers his own humanity. With *Native Son*, Wright introduces the pain of racism and its detrimental impact on black psyches.

Wright's autobiography, *Black Boy,* was published in 1945. He moved to Paris in 1947 after making a short visit two years earlier. He joined a number of other writers and artists who found Paris more accepting of black talent. In Paris, he continued writing novels and nonfiction on international politics, particularly anticolonialism.

PUBLICATIONS
Uncle Tom's Children (1938)
Native Son (1940)
White Man, Listen (1957)
Eight Men (1961)
Twelve Million Black Voices (1969)

FURTHER READING
Fabre, Michael. *The World of Richard Wright*. Jackson: University of Mississippi Press, 1985.
Felgar, Robert. *Richard Wright*. Boston: Twayne, 1980.
Kinnamon, Kenneth, and Michael Fabre, eds. *Conversations with Richard Wright*. Jackson: University Press of Mississippi, 1993.
Urban, Joan. *Richard Wright*. New York: Chelsea House, 1989.
Walker, Margaret. *Richard Wright, Daemonic Genius: A Portrait of the Man, A Critical Look at His Work*. New York: Warner, 1988.

Young, Andrew

CIVIL RIGHTS ACTIVIST, POLITICIAN, DIPLOMAT

Born: October 23, 1932
New Orleans, Louisiana

Young grew up in an affluent family in New Orleans, the son of Daisy Fuller, a teacher, and Andrew Jackson Young, Jr., a dentist. He graduated from high school at 15, then studied biology at Howard University. He had planned to be a dentist, like his father, but later decided to study theology at the Hartford Seminary in Connecticut. Young was ordained as a minister of the United Church of Christ in 1955.

While serving as a pastor in the small rural towns of Marion, Alabama, and Thomasville and Beachton, Georgia, Young participated in one of the first voter registration drives in that region. Between 1957 and 1961, he served as assistant director of the National Council of Churches in New York City. Returning to Georgia to work with a voter education program for the United Church of Christ, Young eventually joined the Southern Christian Leadership Conference (SCLC), where he coordinated fund raising and ran their voter registration program. During these years, Young became a close adviser to the head of the SCLC, Martin Luther King, Jr. Young served as executive director of the organization from 1964 until 1968 and as executive vice-president until 1970.

Young left his full-time work at the SCLC to pursue a career in electoral politics. He won a seat in the House of Representatives in

1972, where he was an effective legislator, and was re-elected for two subsequent terms. In 1976 he resigned his congressional seat when the new President, Jimmy Carter, selected Young to serve as the U.S. ambassador to the United Nations. At the UN, Young was an outspoken critic of the apartheid government in South Africa, and consistently addressed the concerns of African and other "Third World" nations. In 1979, he was forced to resign from his UN post when newspapers reported that he had held secret negotiations with members of the Palestine Liberation Organization, in violation of a U.S. boycott of the organization.

From 1982 until 1990, Young served as mayor of Atlanta. By helping to attract investment in the city by entrepreneurs and developers, he accelerated its development into a major financial hub and convention center. Yet many blacks criticized him for ignoring the city's African-American population, and especially the black poor. Since 1990, he has worked for an international consulting firm. Young also led the committee that brought the 1996 Olympic Games to Atlanta.

PUBLICATION
An Easy Burden: The Civil Rights Movement and the Transformation of America (1996)

FURTHER READING
Gardner, Carl. *Andrew Young: A Biography*. New York: Drake, 1978.
Haskins, James. *Andrew Young: Man with a Mission*. New York: Lothrop, Lee & Shepard, 1979.
Raines, Howell. *My Soul Is Rested: Movement Days in the Deep South Remembered*. New York: Putnam, 1977.

Young, Coleman

LABOR ORGANIZER, POLITICIAN

Born: May 24, 1918
Tuscaloosa, Alabama

Coleman Young grew up in Huntsville, Alabama, until his family moved north in the 1920s to escape white violence and find better employment. During the 1930s and 40s, Young apprenticed as an electrician at the Ford Motor Company, assembled cars on the Ford assembly line, and worked for the U.S. Postal Service. Drafted into the Air Force, he served with the Tuskegee Airmen during World War II as a bombardier-navigator. In an early political protest, Young and a group of black officers were arrested for demanding service at a "whites only" officers club, forcing the Air Force to integrate the club.

Young was a union organizer for the United Automobile Workers (UAW) and later organized workers in the Postal Service. Eventually becoming a full-time organizer for the radical wing of the Congress of Industrial Organizations (CIO), he pushed the organization to defend the rights of black workers and to support Detroit's civil rights movement. The job made Young a very visible figure in county politics.

In 1950, Young helped found the Detroit-based National Negro Labor Conference (NNLC), a group committed to protecting civil rights at the workplace. Among other actions, the NNLC helped force Sears to hire black clerks in their Detroit stores. The U.S. attorney general accused the NNLC of being a "communist front," in part because Young openly welcomed the support offered by members of the Michigan Communist party. The UAW quickly distanced itself from both Young and the NNLC. When a congressional committee demanded that Young testify about his political work, he refused to identify his fellow activists, an act of defiance that only increased his stature in Detroit's black community.

Blacklisted from working in Detroit's auto industry, Young sold insurance in the late 1950s and became active in the Democratic party. He was elected to the state senate in 1964. Young's vocal support for labor unions, open housing legislation, and school desegregation made him increasingly popular in Detroit's black community. In 1973, he was elected mayor of Detroit by the city's new black majority, after campaigning on a promise to reform the mostly white and notoriously racist police force. Between 1967 and 1978, the number of blacks on the force increased from 5 to 35 percent. Young also promoted citizen involvement in policing and brought more African Americans into municipal government.

Throughout his years in office, Young helped sponsor a number of economic partnerships between big business, organized labor, and community groups. These arrangements brought millions of dollars in private and state funds to Detroit yet could not stem the tide of industrial decline. By the time he left office in 1992, many accused Young of caving in to the demands of big business.

PUBLICATION
Hard Stuff: The Autobiography of Coleman Young (1994)

FURTHER READING
Rich, Wilbur. *Coleman Young and Detroit Politics: From Social Activist to Power Broker.* Detroit: Wayne State University Press, 1989.

The central panel of this 19th-century engraving illustrates the hopes most slaves had after emancipation—enjoying a happy and secure family life and a home of their own.

A poster produced in 1949 by the NAACP to commemorate the 50th anniversary of its founding.

MUSEUMS AND HISTORIC SITES RELATED TO THE HISTORY OF AFRICAN AMERICANS

◇ ◇ ◇

Alabama

Alabama Sports Hall of Fame
2150 Civic Center Boulevard
Birmingham, AL 35203
205-323-6665

Alabama's most famous athletes, including Joe Louis and Jesse Owens, are celebrated through film, video, and memorabilia.

Birmingham Civil Rights Institute
520 16th Street North
Birmingham, AL 35203
205-328-9696

Exhibits presenting the history of the civil rights struggle since the early 20th century.

George Washington Carver Museum and Tuskegee Institute
National Historic Site
1212 Old Montgomery Road
Tuskegee, AL 36087
334-727-3200

Located in "The Oaks" home of Booker T. Washington, exhibits artifacts associated with the scientist George Washington Carver and the educator Booker T. Washington.

See additional entries under Iowa *and* Virginia *for Carver and Washington, respectively.*

City Museum
355 Government Street
334-434-7569
Mobile, AL 36602

Interpreting the history of Mobile, the museum incorporates the stories of all the city's citizens, including African Americans.

Civil Rights Memorial
400 Washington Avenue
Montgomery, AL 36104
334-264-0286

Designed by Maya Lin to honor the men and women who died in the struggle for racial equality in the United States.

W. C. Handy Home, Museum, and Library
620 W. College Street
Florence, AL 35360
205-760-6434

Artifacts and memorabilia related to the life and work of W. C. Handy (1873–1958), an American composer and musician whose work includes "The Memphis Blues" (1911).

See Handy entry under Tennessee.

Old Depot Museum
Water Avenue
Selma, AL 36701
334-874-2197

Interprets Alabama's history through artifacts and photographs, including the Kepp Collection, which depicts the lives of 19th-century African-American laborers.

Edmund Pettus Bridge and Historical Marker
Highway 80
Selma, AL 36703

Marks the site of the historic and violent confrontation of the Selma-to-Montgomery Voting Rights March in 1965.

National African American Archives
64 Martin Luther King Avenue

Mobile, AL 36603
334-433-8511

Exhibits on multiple aspects of African-American history and culture, locally as well as nationally, and the African diaspora.

16th Street Baptist Church
1530 Sixth Avenue North
Birmingham, AL 35203
205-251-9402

A nationally prominent church, it served as the local headquarters for the civil rights movement in the 1960s and was the site of a Ku Klux Klan bombing on September 15, 1965, that took the lives of four young girls.

Arkansas

Central High School
1500 Park Street
Little Rock, AR 72202
501-376-4751

A historical marker on the school grounds recalls the controversial events around the desegregation process in the 1950s brought about by the 1954 U.S. Supreme Court decision in *Brown* v. *Board of Education.*

Ethnic Minorities Memorabilia Association Museum
P.O. Box 55
Washington, AR 71862
501-983-2891

Dedicated to regional African-American history and culture, collections can be viewed by appointment.

Isaac Hathaway Fine Arts Center
University of Arkansas at Pine Bluff
1200 North University Drive
Pine Bluff, AR 71601
501-543-8236

Presents an exhibit called "Keepers of the Spirit" chronicling the history of the school, of which black Arkansans have been a part since the early 1800s. The center also has an art gallery.

Arizona

Pima Air and Space Museum
6000 East Valencia Road
Tucson, AZ 85706
520-574-0462

Exhibits on the development of air and space travel incorporate the contributions and roles of African Americans, including the Tuskegee Airmen.

California

African American Historical and Cultural Society
Fort Mason Center
Building C Room 165
San Francisco, CA 94123
415-441-0640

Features an exhibit on the Buffalo Soldiers and other displays relating to African-American history in the West.

African American Museum and Library at Oakland
5606 San Pablo Ave
Oakland, CA 94608
510-597-5053

The museum holds exhibits on African-American history with an emphasis on California and the West.

African American Museum of Fine Arts
3025 Fir Street
San Diego, CA 92104
619-696-7799

A multidisciplinary institution sponsoring outreach programs, performance art, and displays of its permanent collection of fine art.

California Afro-American Museum
600 State Drive
Exposition Park
Los Angeles, CA 90037
213-744-7432

Displays art and historical artifacts relating to African-American culture.

Colorado

Black American West Museum and Heritage Center
3091 California Street
Denver, CO 80205
303-292-2566

Housed in the home of Justina Ford, the first black female doctor in Colorado, the museum explores various aspects of black heritage in the West, including cowboys and military history.

Connecticut

Prudence Crandall Museum
Junction of Routes 14 & 169
Canterbury, CT 06331
203-546-9916

The historic house of Prudence Crandall (1803–90), who opened a school for African-American girls despite intense opposition; the museum interprets her life and work as well as related issues.

New Haven Colony Historical Society
114 Whitney Avenue
New Haven, CT 06510
203-562-4183

Located in an 18th-century historic house, the society explores the social, cultural, political, and ethnic-racial history of New Haven; holds material related to the mutiny of African slaves aboard the slave ship *Amistad* in 1839.

Harriet Beecher Stowe Center
77 Forest Street
Hartford, CT 06105
203-522-9258

Located in the 19th-century Nook Farm neighborhood; items about slavery, abolition, and African-American history.

See Stowe entry under Ohio.

Delaware

John Dickinson Plantation
Kitts Hummock Road
Dover, DE 19901
302-739-3277

An 18th-century plantation whose slaves were freed in 1785 and on which many continued to work as free laborers. The site has a special tour focusing on African-American life.

District of Columbia

Anacostia Museum
1901 Fort Place, SE
Washington, DC 20020
202-287-3306

Devoted to the identification, documentation, and preservation of African-American experience in the Upper South; presents exhibits and programs examining history and contemporary social issues.

Bethune Museum and Archives
1318 Vermont Avenue, NW
Washington, DC 20005
202-332-1233

Housed in the former residence of the educator and political activist Mary McLeod Bethune (1875–1955), the museum provides exhibits and programs related to black women's history.

See Bethune entry under Florida.

Frederick Douglass National Historic Site
1411 W Street, SE
Washington, DC 20020
202-426-5961

The historic home of Douglass holds letters, writings, and documents related to his life.

See Douglass entry under New York.

Prince Hall Masonic Temple
1000 U Street, NW
Washington, DC 20001
202-483-3174

Named for Prince Hall, who organized the first black lodge of Freemasons in America in 1775, this building, completed in 1929, served as home to the Grand Lodge of the District of Columbia.

Howard University, Gallery of Art
2455 6th Street, NW
Washington, DC 20059
202-806-7070

Part of the historically black college, the gallery exhibits African, African-American, and American art.

Mt. Zion United Methodist Church
1334 29th Street, NW
Washington, DC 20007

As the oldest black church in Georgetown (tracing its history to 1816), the church attests to the deep roots of the African-American community in the historic district.

National Museum of American History
Smithsonian Institution
14th Street & Constitution Avenue, NW
Washington, DC 20560
202-357-2700

Dedicated to portraying the nation's heritage, this museum features exhibits on the migration of African Americans to the North in the 1910s and the civil rights movement, holds a major collection of the American musician Duke Ellington (1899–1974), and frequently presents programs related to black history.

National Museum of African Art
Smithsonian Institution
950 Independence Avenue, NW
Washington, DC 20560
202-357-3600

Devoted to the collection, exhibition, and study of African art, the museum displays traditional and contemporary works.

Florida

Historic George Adderly Conch House
5550 Overseas Highway
Marathon, FL 33050
305-743-9100

The restored house of Adderly, a Bahamian who was a prominent and leading townsman of the early–20th-century African-American settlement.

African American Caribbean Cultural Center
614 North Andrews
Fort Lauderdale, FL 33311
954-467-5881

Exhibits of art, crafts, and history and theater programs explore the cultural evolution and exchange of black Americans and Caribbean immigrants.

Mary McLeod Bethune Foundation
Bethune-Cookman College
640 Mary McLeod Bethune Boulevard
Daytona Beach, FL 32114
904-255-1401, ext. 200

At the college established by the educator and civil rights activist, the foundation's gallery relates the history of the college and Bethune's work. The Fine Arts Building features an art gallery of African culture.

See Bethune entry under District of Columbia.

Black Archives, Research Center, and Museum
Carnegie Library
Florida A&M University
Tallahassee, FL 32399
904-599-3020

Holds an assortment of material culture relating to the African-American experience, ranging from the African diaspora to civil protest and pop culture.

Black Heritage Museum

William A. Chapman
   Elementary School
27190 Southwest 140 Avenue
Narango, FL 33032
305-245-1055

Holds various African artifacts, such as masks, textiles, books, and dolls related to black heritage around the world; by appointment.

Julee Cottage Museum
Historic Pensacola Village
120 Church Street
Pensacola, FL 32501
904-444-8905

A history museum dedicated to African-American heritage in West Florida. Housed in an antebellum Creole-style cottage.

Kingsley Plantation
11676 Palmetto Avenue
Jacksonville, FL 32226
904-251-3537

The oldest remaining example of an 18th-century cotton and sugarcane plantation in Florida. Remains of the slave cabins, service structures, and the main house can be visited.

Museum of African American Art
13 North Florida Avenue
Tampa, FL 33602
813-272-2466

Dedicated to the presentation of African-American art.

Tallahassee Museum of History and Natural Science
3945 Museum Drive
Tallahassee, FL 32310
904-575-8684

Exhibits relating to African-American life include restored structures of a 19th-century church and schoolhouse.

◇ ◇ ◇
Georgia

The APEX Museum
135 Auburn Avenue, NE
Atlanta, GA 30303
404-521-2739

APEX (the African American Panoramic Experience), located in the Martin Luther King, Jr., National Historic District, features tours and exhibits related to African and African-American art and life.

Atlanta History Center
130 West Paces Ferry Road,
   NW
Atlanta, GA 30305
404-814-4000

A 32-acre property including historic exhibits and houses encompassing the history of Atlanta, the Civil War, and African Americans.

The Herndon Home
587 University Place, NW
Atlanta, GA 30314
404-581-9813

The home of Alonzo Herndon, a former slave who became Atlanta's first black millionaire. The area's history is interpreted through the life of the Herndon family.

Martin Luther King, Jr. Center for Nonviolent Social Change
449 Auburn Avenue, NE
Atlanta, GA 30312
404-524-1956

A history museum and educational center; visitors can view the furnishings of the King family, Dr. King's crypt, personal effects, and memorabilia donated by the public.

Martin Luther King, Jr. National Historic Site
450 Auburn Avenue, NE
Atlanta, GA 30312
404-331-3920

The neighborhood in which Dr. King grew up, including his birthplace, boyhood home, and church.

King-Tisdell Cottage
The Beach Institute
502 East Harris Street
Savannah, GA 34101
912-234-8000

History and culture of
Savannah and the Sea Islands;
offers a Negro History Trail
tour.

**Morgan County African
American Museum**
156 Academy Street
Madison, GA 30650
706-342-9191

In its mission to preserve and
present the experience of
African Americans in the rural
South, the museum explores
black history in the context of
slavery and Reconstruction
through its local and family
history.

**Tubman African American
Museum**
340 Walnut Street
Macon, GA 31201
912-743-8544

Named for Harriet Tubman,
hero of the Underground
Railroad, the museum is
devoted to African-American
history, culture, and art.

Illinois

**Du Sable Museum of
African American History**
740 E. 56th Place
Washington Park
Chicago, IL 60637
312-947-0600

Named after Jean Baptiste
Point Du Sable, a Haitian
trader who was the first per-
manent settler in Chicago.
Exhibits on "Blacks in Early
Illinois" and various topics in
African-American history and
culture.

The Peace Museum
314 West Institute Place
Chicago, IL 60610
312-440-1860

Dedicated to issues of political struggle and peace,
exhibits incorporate the civil
rights movement in America
and Martin Luther King, Jr.'s
peacemaking role.

Indiana

Crispus Attucks Museum
1140 Martin Luther King, Jr.,
　Street
Indianapolis, IN 46202
317-226-4611

Located in the Crispus
Attucks High School and
named after the free Black-
Indian who died in the Boston
Massacre in 1770. Presents
the history of the school as
well as local, state, and
national African-American
history.

Levi Coffin House
North Main Street
Fountain City, IN 47341
317-847-2432

This restored home of the
Quaker Levi Coffin was a stop
on the Underground Railroad.
Coffin was active in setting up
networks among whites across
several states to smuggle
slaves to freedom.

Freetown Village
Indiana State Museum
202 North Alabama Street
Indianapolis, IN 46204
317-232-1634/631-1870

An exhibit area of a
"Freetown Village" explores
the post-emancipation experience of African Americans
through living history performances. Call in advance for
performance schedules.

Lick Creek Settlement
Hoosier National Forest
    Headquarters
811 Constitution Avenue
Bedford, IN 47421
812-275-5987

An early African-American
settlement, which began in
1815. Within the National
Forest are graves and rem-
nants of the settlers' church.

**Madam Walker Urban Life
Center**
617 Indiana Avenue
Indianapolis, IN 46202
317-236-2099

Housed in the former headquarters of Madam C. J.
Walker (1867–1919), the first
self-made black female millionaire in the United States.
The center offers perfor-
mance programs and tours
with advance notice.

Iowa

Carver Museum
Warren County Fairgrounds,
    Highway 92W
Indianola, IA 50125
515-961-6031

The museum displays the scientist George Washington
Carver's experiencés as a
young man at nearby Simpson
College, where he studied art
and botany.

See Carver entry under
Alabama.

Jordan House Museum
2001 Fuller Road
West Des Moines, IA 50265
515-225-1286

The former home of a state
senator, James C. Jordan, who
assisted the Underground
Railroad. Highlights Iowa's
role in abolition activities.

**University of Iowa Art
Museum**
150 North Riverside Drive
Iowa City, IA 52242
319-335-1727

Presents an extensive collection of African art and
artifacts.

Kansas

**Adaire Cabin/John Brown
Museum**
John Brown Memorial Park
Tenth and Main Streets
Osawatamie, KS 66064
913-755-4384

In honor of the militant abolitionist, the museum explores
the 1850s period known as
"bleeding Kansas" because of
the violent confrontations
between antislavery and
proslavery settlers.

*See Harpers Ferry entry
under* West Virginia.

**Fort Larned National
Historic Site**
Route 156
Larned, KS 67550
316-285-6911

Features presentations on the
Buffalo Soldiers among the
exhibits interpreting the fort,
which was built in 1860.

**Elizabeth Watkins
Community Museum**
1047 Massachusetts Street
Lawrence, KS 66044
913-841-4109

Explores the town's local history and holds a statue of a
famous resident, the writer
Langston Hughes (1902–67).

Kentucky

Kentucky Derby Museum
704 Central Avenue
Louisville, KY 40201
502-637-1111

Spotlights African Americans
in the world of horse racing
since the 19th century with
the exhibit "African-
Americans in Thoroughbred
Racing."

J. B. Speed Art Museum
2035 South Third Street
Louisville, KY 40201
502-636-2893

Displays a variety of artifacts
from Africa.

◇ ◇ ◇
Louisiana

Arna Bontemps African American Museum and Cultural Art Center
1327 Third Street
Alexandria, LA 71301
318-473-4692

Located in the home of Arna Bontemps (1902–73), an African-American writer whose work depicts African-American life and heritage. The museum explores local and national history.

Louis Armstrong Park
901 North Rampart Street at
    St. Anne Street
New Orleans, LA 70116

Named in honor of the great musician, located near the musical scene of his youth, the park features a sculpture of Armstrong (1900–71) created by the sculptor Elizabeth Catlett.

Melrose Plantation
Highway 119
Melrose, LA 71452
318-379-0055

The vast estate of a freed slave, Marie Thérèse Coincoin, and her descendants. Eight buildings have been restored and are open to the public.

◇ ◇ ◇
Maryland

African Art Museum of Maryland
5430 Vantage Point Road
Town Center
Columbia, MD 21044
410-730-7105

A museum of traditional African art, including household items and musical instruments, it interprets various aspects of African and African-American culture.

Baltimore's Only Black American Museum
1769 Carswell Street
Baltimore, MD 21218

Contemporary art gallery and black cultural center.

Banneker Douglass Museum
84 Franklin Street
Annapolis, MD 21401
410-974-2893

Interprets Maryland history through its collections of African-American historical and cultural artifacts.

The Eubie Blake National Museum and Cultural Center
34 Market Place
Baltimore, MD 21202
410-625-3880

Named for the American ragtime pianist and composer James Herbert "Eubie" Blake (1883–1983), the museum presents exhibits on American and African-American culture.

Great Blacks in Wax Museum
1601 E. North Avenue
Baltimore, MD 21213
410-563-3404

Exhibits highlighting African-American history from ancient Africa to the present.

James E. Lewis Museum of Art
Morgan State University
Coldspring Lane and Hillen
    Road
Baltimore, MD 21239
410-319-303

Displays collections of traditional African art, art from New Guinea, and art by African Americans.

Lovely Lane Museum
Lovely Lane Church Building
2200 St. Paul Street
Baltimore, MD 21218
410-889-4458

Interpreting the history of the United Methodist Church in the United States, it displays some African-American material.

◇ ◇ ◇
Massachusetts

Boston African American Historic Site
African Meeting House
46 Joy Street
Boston, MA 02114
617-742-5415

Housed in the 1806 African Meeting House, which is the oldest extant black church in the United States. Explores the history of African Americans in New England during the 19th century and administers the "Black Heritage Trail" tour.

Harriet Tubman House
566 Columbus Avenue
Boston, MA 02118
617-536-8610

A museum about Harriet Tubman and the history of the Underground Railroad.

Museum of the National Center of Afro-American Artists
300 Walnut Avenue
Roxbury, MA 02119
617-442-8614

Located in a historic 19th-century Victorian mansion, the center presents contemporary art by African Americans.

◇ ◇ ◇
Michigan

Joe Louis Sculptures
Jefferson Avenue
Detroit, MI 48226

Within a few blocks of each other along Jefferson Avenue are two sculptures honoring the great boxing champion.

Motown Historical Museum
2648 West Grand Boulevard
Detroit, MI 48208
313-875-2264

History and memorabilia related to the Motown Record Company, which operated between 1959 and 1972.

Museum of African American History
301 Frederick Douglass Boulevard
Detroit, MI 48202
313-833-9800

Art, photographs, and objects pertaining to prominent African Americans of Detroit and national African-American history and culture.

Your Heritage House
110 E. Ferry Avenue
Detroit, MI 48202
313-871-1667

Devoted to learning through the arts, the center caters to young people of diverse cultures by providing programs and displays.

◇ ◇ ◇
Minnesota

Minnesota Museum of American Art
75 West 5th Street
St. Paul, MN 55102
612-292-4355

Dedicated to the collection and exhibition of American art, the museum has a multicultural focus and actively collects and presents African-American artworks.

Dred Scott Memorial
Historic Fort Snelling
Highway 55
St. Paul, MN 55111
612-726-1171

Outside the historic antebellum fort is a statue of Dred Scott, recalling the controversial U.S. Supreme Court decision of 1857.

◇ ◇ ◇
Mississippi

Delta Blues Museum
114 Delta Avenue
Clarkesdale, MS 38614
601-627-6820

Permanent and changing exhibits, programs, and an annual festival explore Delta Blues music and its origins.

Missouri

Black Archives of Mid-America
2033 Vine Street
Kansas City, MO 64108
816-483-1300

A museum and research center dedicated to local and national African-American culture.

Vaughn Cultural Center
525 North Grand Street
Saint Louis, MO 63103
314-535-93227

Library and gallery display material culture and art related to African-American history.

Montana

Historical Museum at Fort Missoula
Building 322, Fort Missoula
Missoula, MT 59801
406-728-3476

Presenting the history of the former U.S. Army fort, opened in 1872; includes the duties and activities of black troopers.

Nebraska

Great Plains Black Museum
2213 Lake Street
Omaha, NE 68110
402-345-2212

Exhibitions on African-American settlers, cowboys, and women of the Great Plains; tours of Underground Railroad stops.

New Hampshire

Hood Museum of Art
Dartmouth College
Hanover, NH 03755
603-646-2808

The museum features a collection of African art and artifacts, including masks, statues, and staffs.

New Jersey

Afro-American Historical Society Museum
1841 Kennedy Boulevard
Jersey City, NJ 07305
201-547-5262

Interprets African-American history in New Jersey, covering civil rights, fraternal organizations, churches, domestic life, and music.

Newark Museum
49 Washington Street
Newark, NJ 07101
201-596-6550

The art and science museum of Newark regularly incorporates African-American artists in its interpretation of American art and holds in its collection works by Jacob Lawrence, Romare Bearden, and Henry Ossawa Tanner, among others.

New Mexico

Folsom Museum
Main Street
Folsom, NM 88419
505-278-2122

Exhibits on the Folsom prehistoric man discovery and its discoverer, the former slave and cowboy George McJunkin.

Fort Selden State Monument
Interstate 25, Exit 19
Radium Springs, NM 88054
505-526-8911

Military history and artifacts including photographs and a statue of the Buffalo Soldiers.

New York

Black Fashion Museum
155 West 126th Street
New York, NY 10027
212-666-1320

Displays the history of African-American designers and fashions from the 19th century to the present.

Brooklyn Historical Society
128 Pierrepont Street
Brooklyn, NY 11201
718-624-0890

The society has a research library and museum with temporary and long-term exhibits interpreting Brooklyn's cultural and social history, including the African-American community.

Frederick Douglass Grave and Monument
Mount Hope Cemetery
Rochester, NY 14620
716-473-2755

At the historic cemetery, tourists may visit the graves of Frederick Douglass and several other renowned Rochester residents.

See Douglass entry under District of Columbia.

Historic Talman Building
25 East Main Street
Rochester, NY 14614
716-546-3960

Located in the city's historic district, the building where Frederick Douglass ran his abolitionist newspaper, *The North Star,* and which was a stop on the Underground Railroad.

Office of Public Education and Interpretation of the African Burial Ground
U.S. Custom House, Room 239
6 World Trade Center
New York, NY 10048
212-432-5707

Historical slide presentation and tours related to the excavation of an African burial ground. Thousands of artifacts and hundreds of skeletal remains have been uncovered in the middle of Manhattan.

Society for the Preservation of Weeksville & Bedford-Stuyvesant History
1698 Bergen Street
Brooklyn, NY 11213
718-756-5250

The society maintains properties and material culture of the 19th-century African-American community.

Studio Museum in Harlem
144 West 125th Street
New York, NY 10026
212-864-4500

Dedicated to artists of color, presents African-American, Caribbean, African, and Hispanic, and contemporary art.

Harriet Tubman Home
180 South Street
Auburn, NY 13021
315-252-2081

The first home of the former slave and abolitionist, which later became a home for the aged; a tour relates the life and work of Harriet Tubman.

North Carolina

Afro-American Cultural Center
401 North Myers Street
Charlotte, NC 28202
704-374-1565

Housed in a historic church building, the center displays art and provides performance programs related to African and African-American culture.

Charlotte Hawkins Brown Memorial State Historic Site
6135 Burlington Road
Sedalia, NC 27342
910-449-4846

The Palmer Memorial Institute was a school for African Americans founded by Brown (1883–1961), an educator, author, and active clubwoman, in 1902. Tours and exhibits include an audiovisual presentation of the school's history and Brown's contribution to education in the South.

Greensboro Historical Museum
130 Summit Avenue
Greensboro, NC 27401
910-373-2043

Interprets local history, incorporating the ethnic and African-American presence; of note is a display of the historic civil rights sit-in at the Woolworth lunch counter in the 1960s.

Stagville Preservation Center
5825 Old Oxford Highway
Bahama, NC 27503
919-620-0120

A late 18th- and 19th-century tobacco plantation that held several slave communities. Visitors can view original two-story slave dwellings, artifacts, and a barn built by slaves at Horton Grove.

See entry under Alabama.

◇ ◇ ◇
Ohio

African American Museum
1765 Crawford Road
Cleveland, OH 44106
216-791-1700

Museum of African-American heritage exploring the people and culture through various artifacts.

Payne Cemetery
Wayne National Forest
219 Columbus Road
Athens, OH 45701
614-592-6644

The gravesite of U.S. colored troops who served in the Civil War is all that remains of the early-19th-century African-American community. Ongoing research reveals the stories of several families.

National Afro-American Museum and Cultural Center
1350 Brush Row Road
Wilberforce, OH 45384
513-376-4944

Museum of black history and culture, featuring the permanent exhibit "From Victory to Freedom: Afro-American Life in the Fifties."

Harriet Beecher Stowe House
2950 Gilbert Avenue
Cincinnati, OH 45206
513-632-5120

The home of the Beecher family is named for the author of the antislavery work *Uncle Tom's Cabin* and relates the history of the abolition movement.

See Stowe entry under Connecticut.

Oberlin College
Carnegie Building
101 North Professor Street
Oberlin, OH 44074
216-775-8121

Pushed by the strong abolitionist sentiment in the area, Oberlin College opened its doors to African Americans and women in the 1830s. Several sites on the campus relate the history of active black and white abolitionists.

◇ ◇ ◇
Oklahoma

Boley Historic District
c/o Boley Chamber of
    Commerce
125 South Pecan Street
Boley, OK 74829
918-667-3477

Originally an all-black town
founded in 1905, the Boley
Historic District is a National
Historic Landmark.

Greenwood Cultural
Center
322 North Greenwood
Tulsa, OK 74120
918-583-4545

Documents history of Tulsa's
African-American community
through photographs and art.

◇ ◇ ◇
Oregon

Portland Museum of Art
1219 Southwest Park
Portland, OR 97205
503-226-2811

Within its collection there are
paintings by local African-
American artists, works by
Jacob Lawrence, and art
pieces from Cameroon.

◇ ◇ ◇
Pennsylvania

Afro-American Historical
and Cultural Museum
701 Arch Street
Philadelphia, PA 19106
215-574-0380/0381

Exhibits on black history in
Pennsylvania since the colonial period, African sculpture
and artifacts, and African-
American art.

Father Divine Shrine
1622 Spring Mill Road
Gladwyne, PA 19035
610-525-5598

Shrine to George Baker
(c.1880–1965), founder of the
racially integrated Peace
Mission Movement.

Mother Bethel African
Methodist Episcopal
Church
419 South Sixth Street
Philadelphia, PA 19147
215-925-0616

Founded by Bishop Richard
Allen (1760–1831) in 1794 to
protest segregated seating in
white Methodist churches.
The church museum is dedicated to the history of the
church and Allen's achievements.

◇ ◇ ◇
Rhode Island

Haffenreffer Museum of
Anthropology
300 Tower Street
Bristol, RI 02809
401-253-8388

In addition to the anthropo-
logical artifacts of the
Americas, Mideast, Asia, and
the Pacific, the museum
maintains an African collection that includes, sculptures,
woodcarvings, and masks.

Black Regiment Park
Route 114
Portsmouth, RI 02871

A memorial commemorates
the free African Americans
and former slaves who served
in the Battle of Rhode Island
during the American
Revolution.

Rhode Island Black
Heritage Society
46 Aborn Street
Providence, RI 02903
401-751-3490

The museum provides tours,
lectures, exhibits, and other
programs on the history of
African Americans in Rhode
Island.

South Carolina

Avery Research Center for African-American History and Culture
125 Bull Street
Charleston, SC 29424
803-727-2009

A museum and archive presenting history of the lowcountry and African heritage.

Columbia Historic Foundation
1601 Richland Street
Columbia, SC 29201
803-252-1770

Dedicated to identifying and preserving the history of Columbia, the foundation administers the "African-American Heritage Site Tour" featuring 50 sites.

I. P. Stanback Museum and Planetarium
South Carolina State
    University
300 College Street, NE
Orangeburg, SC 29117
803-536-7174

African and African-American art of the 20th century.

Mann-Simons Cottage
1403 Richland Street
Columbia, SC 29201
803-929-7691

A historic house that was owned by a free African-American midwife, Celia Mann, in antebellum Columbia.

Penn Center
110 Martin Luther King Drive
St. Helena Island, SC 29920
803-838-2432

A national historic district with a museum that interprets local African-American history.

South Dakota

Adams Museum
54 Sherman Street
Deadwood, SD 57732
605-578-1714

Promoting the history of the Black Hills area, the museum highlights the presence of African Americans through photographs. The museum also holds West African artifacts.

Shrine to Music Museum
Clark and Yale Streets
Vermillion, SD 57069
605-677-5306

In this museum dedicated to the history of musical instruments, visitors will find African and African-American instruments and exhibits on traditions of African-American music.

Allen Chapel A.M.E. Church
508 Cedar Street
Yankton, SD 57078
605-665-1449

Named for the leader Richard Allen, the church was established by the African-American community in the 1880s and is the oldest black church in the state.

Tennessee

Chattanooga African-American Museum
200 E. Martin Luther King
    Boulevard
Chattanooga, TN 37403
423-267-1076

Displays local African-American history and memorabilia of the blues singer Bessie Smith (1894–1937).

Alex Haley House Museum
200 South Church Street
Henning, TN 38041
901-738-2240

Located in the home built by Haley's grandfather. Presents local history and displays memorabilia of the author Alex Haley (1921–92), who is buried on the grounds.

W. C. Handy Blues Museum
352 Beale Street
Memphis, TN 38103
901-396-3914

Located in the historic district of Memphis, the former family home of the great blues musician and writer W. C. Handy (1873–1958); displays memorabilia tracing his career.

See Handy entry under Alabama.

National Civil Rights Museum
450 Mulberry Street
Memphis, TN 38103
901-521-9699

History of the civil rights movement. Located in the former Loraine Motel, site of Dr. Martin Luther King, Jr.'s, assassination.

Texas

African American Museum
3536 Grand Avenue
Dallas, TX 75210
214-565-9026

A museum about African Americans of the Southwest; features an exhibit on African-American folk art and an archive that includes material about black women's history.

George Washington Carver Museum
1165 Angelina Street
Austin, TX 78702
512-472-4809

Named for the scientist whose work helped African-American sharecroppers and farmers in the South, the museum interprets local and national African-American history and African heritage.

Utah

Calvary Baptist Church
532 East 700 South Street
Salt Lake City, UT 84102
801-355-1025

The oldest black Baptist church in Utah displays its collection of African-American art and artifacts.

Fort Douglas Museum
32 Potter Street
Salt Lake City, UT 84113
801-588-5188

Located in the original 19th-century fort, the museum includes exhibits on Buffalo Soldier regiments.

Trinity A.M.E. Church
230 600 South Street
Salt Lake City, UT 84102
801-531-7374

The first African-American church to be erected in Utah.

Vermont

Rokeby Museum
Route 7
Ferrisburgh, VT 05456
802-877-3406

The 18th- and 19th-century home of Rowland E. Robinson, an American writer whose parents were Quaker abolitionists, was a stop on the Underground Railroad.

Virginia

Alexandria Black History Resource Center
638 N. Alfred Street
Alexandria, VA 22314
703-838-4356

Local and national African-American history, exhibits, lectures, film presentations, and walking tours.

Arlington House, The Robert E. Lee Memorial
Arlington National Cemetery
Arlington, VA 22101
703-557-0614

A historic house museum built in 1802, where Robert E. Lee resided in the 1860s; features slave quarters.

Black Civil War Veterans' Memorial
Elmwood Cemetery
238 East Princess Anne Road
Norfolk, VA 23510
804-441-2576

The only African-American soldiers' memorial in the South honoring Union veterans.

Black History Museum
00 Clay Street
Richmond, VA 23219
804-780-90933

African-American history and culture of Virginia.

Carter's Grove, Colonial Williamsburg Foundation
134 North Henry Street
Williamsburg, VA 23185
804-229-1000

This site includes re-created 18th-century slave quarters and features extensive interpretation of a colonial tobacco plantation.

Fort Monroe and Casemate Museum
Building 20, Bernard Road
Fort Monroe, VA 23651
804-727-3391

Located in the early–19th-century fort where Major General Benjamin Butler declared runaway slaves "contraband" in 1861 and African-American refugees served the Union cause.

Gadsby's Museum
134 North Royal Street
Alexandria, VA 22314
703-838-4242

A tavern run by the 18th-century slave trader, John Gadsby; the museum integrates historical interpretation of African-American slavery.

Hampton University Museum
Hampton University
Hampton, VA 23668
804-727-5308

The museum holds collections of traditional and contemporary African and African-American art.

Harrison Museum of African American Culture
523 Harrison Avenue, NW
Roanoke, VA 24016
703-345-4818

Housed in the former Harrison School building, a renowned all-black high school from the 1920s to the 1960s; highlights the history of African Americans of the Roanoke Valley and southwest Virginia, and displays work of African-American artists.

Monticello
Route 53
Charlottesville VA 22902
804-984-9808

The estate of Thomas Jefferson was built and maintained with the help of slave labor. Service structures and the excavations of Mulberry Row interpret slave plantation life.

Mount Vernon Estate
George Washington Parkway South
Mount Vernon, VA 22121
703-780-2000

The home of George Washington, with exhibits about 18th-century plantation life, re-created slave quarters, and a slave burial ground.

Newsome House Museum and Cultural Center
2803 Oak Avenue
Newport News, VA 23607
804-247-2360

A community center and museum presenting the African-American history of Newport News and the life of Joseph Thomas Newsome (1869–1942), a respected African-American civic leader.

Maggie Lena Walker National Historic Site
110 1/2 East Leigh Street
Richmond, VA 23219
804-780-1380

The historic home of Maggie Lena Walker (1867–1934), the first woman in the United States to establish and direct a bank, and who was also a publisher and civic leader.

Museum of the Confederacy
1201 East Clay Street
Richmond, VA 23219
804-649-1861

The museum's permanent and changing exhibits focus on the experience of the common soldier as well as the battles and generals of the Civil War. Includes the "White House" of the Confederacy, home of Jefferson Davis from 1861 to 1865.

Booker T. Washington National Monument
12130 Booker T. Washington
   Highway
Hardy, VA 24101
540-721-2094

The birthplace of Booker T. Washington (1854–1915) features a living history tobacco farm. It also highlights Washington as a leading educator of African Americans.

See Washington entry under Alabama.

Valentine Museum
1015 E. Clay Street
Richmond, VA 23219
804-649-0711

A museum of urban history that consistently weaves the African-American presence into its interpretation of Richmond history.

◇ ◇ ◇
Washington

Seattle Art Museum
100 University Street
Seattle, WA 98101
206-625-8900/8913

Among its diverse collection of art from around the world, the museum holds an extensive amount of African art.

◇ ◇ ◇
West Virginia

Harpers Ferry National Historical Park
Filmore Street
Harpers Ferry, WV 25425
304-535-6298

A historic village and park that is the site of the antislavery insurrection led by John Brown in 1859 and the second conference of the Niagara Movement, initiated by W. E. B. Du Bois.

John Brown Wax Museum
High Street
Harpers Ferry, WV 25425
304-535-6342

Portrays the life of the militant abolitionist John Brown.

West Virginia Culture and History
Camp Washington-Carver
Route 1
Clifftop, WV 25831
304-438-3005

The nation's first state 4-H youth camp for African Americans, the camp is now a cultural center promoting black heritage for young people through folklife programs and exhibits.

◇ ◇ ◇
Wisconsin

American Black Holocaust Museum
2233 North Fourth Street
Milwaukee, WI 53212
414-264-2500

Explores slavery and racism in America through books, paintings, photographs, and artifacts.

People gathered at the Washington Monument during the historic March on Washington for Jobs and Freedom in 1963.

Series Index
◇ ◇ ◇

References to illustrations are indicated by page numbers in *italics*.

A

Abbott, Robert, **7:**91-92, 97-98, 102-3, 105, 106-7, 145; **11:**9-10

Abernathy, Ralph David, **9:**39, 59, 105, 106, 122, 138, 159; **11:**10-11

Abolitionists, **5:**15, 17, 19-21, 49

Abolition of slavery, **2:**106-19

Actors, **10:**98-*103*

Adams, Abigail, **2:**113; **3:**31, 32, 42

Adams, John, **2:**108, 110; **3:**121, 124

Adams, Samuel, **3:**26

"Address to the Atheist, An" (Wheatley), **3:***15*

Affirmative action, **8:**71; **10:**7, 56-60, 67-69

Affleck, Thomas, **4:**49

AFL-CIO, **8:**114-15. *See also* American Federation of Labor; Congress of Industrial Organizations

African Blood Brotherhood, **7:**140-41

African Church of Philadelphia, **3:**85

African Episcopal Church of St. Thomas, **3:**86; **4:***91*

African Methodist Episcopal Church, **4:**92; **5:**132; **7:**67, 69

African Methodist Episcopal *Church Review*, **6:**20, 129

African Methodist Episcopal Zion Church (New York), **3:**89

African peoples
  agricultural development, **1:**18
  culture, **1:**21-22
  early civilizations, **1:**18-21
  ethnic groups, **1:**6, 31-33
  fossils of early humans, **1:**16-17
  impact of slave trade, **1:**113-117
  language families, **1:**18
  political divisions, **1:**18-21, 31-32
  tools, **1:**16-17

Afro-American Council, **6:**108

Afrocentrism, **10:***110*-11

Agrarian movements, **6:**53-55

Agricultural activities, **1:**18, 57-58; **3:**100, *101*, 102, 103; **4:**8, 15-17, *24*, 25; **5:**14-15, 40; **6:**16, 17, 52-55; **7:**11-14, 24-25, 31-32, 33-35, 36, 40, 117; **8:**23, 34-35, 52, 54, 58, 73, *74. See also* Farmers, Sharecroppers

Agricultural Adjustment Administration (AAA), **8:**31, 34

Aid to Families with Dependent Children (AFDC), **10:**50

Alabama Christian Movement for Human Rights (ACMHR), **9:**65, 122

Alabama Sharecroppers' Union, **8:**71

Albany Movement (1960s), **9:**99-119

Albornoz, Bartolomé de, **1:**103

Alexander, Will, **8:**48

Ali, Muhammad, **11:**11-12

Ali, Shahrazad, **10:**112, 114

All-black towns, **7:***100*-101; **6:**7, 18, 21, 25-28

Allen, Richard, **3:***81*, 82-86, 105, 110; **11:**12-13

Allston, Adele Pettigru, **4:**59-60

Allston, Robert, **4:**32

Alvará (slave trade decree), **1:**55

American Anti-Slavery Almanac, **4:**116

American Antislavery Society, **4:**99, 101, 108

American Colonization Society, **4:**102, 103, *104*

American Federation of Labor (AFL), **7:**141-42 **8:**55, 57, 68, 69, 90, 107, 114

American Federation of Labor–Congress of Industrial Organizations (AFL-CIO), **8:**114-15

American Missionary Association, **5:**122

American Negro Academy, **6:**104-5

American Negro Labor Council, **8:**116-17

American Revolution. *See* Revolutionary War

An American Dilemma: The Negro Problem and Modern Democracy (Myrdal), **8:**24, 57-58, 79

Anderson, Elijah, **4:**120

Anderson, Marian, **8:**79-81; **11:**13-14

Anderson, Mat, **2:**84

Anderson, Robert, **4:**135

Angelou, Maya, **8:**83; **11:**14-15

Anti-Slavery Alphabet, The, **4:***102*

Anti-Slavery Record, The, **4:**67

Bowen, Amanda, **6**:92-93
Bozales (category of slaves in early Americas), **1**:70-71
Braddock, Gen. Edward, **2**:101
Bradley, Aaron, **5**:71
Bradley, Tom, **10**:74-75; **11**:20-21
Brazil
  colonial slave laws, **1**:45
  emancipation of slaves, **1**:101
  maroon settlement, **1**:97-98
  quilombos settlements, **1**:99
  slave population of, **1**:11-12, 40, 45, 55, 65, 109
  slave revolts in, **1**:97-99
  slave trade to, **1**:55
  sugarcane industry, **1**:51, 53-56, *66*
Br'er Rabbit, **4**:39, 40
Briggs, Cyril, **7**:140-41, 145; **11**:21-22
Briggs v. *Elliott* (1955), **9**:33
Bronzeville (Chicago), **7**:77
Brooks, Preston, **5**:49
Broonzy, Big Bill, **7**:118; **8**:66
Brotherhood of Sleeping Car Porters and Maids, **7**:123, 142; **8**:18, 68, 69, 70, 102; **9**:13, 40
Brown, Clara, **5**:93
Brown, Edgar, **8**:45
Browne, William Washington, **7**:74-75
Brown Fellowship Society, **3**:105; **4**:94
Brown, Hallie Quinn, **6**:124
Brown, Henry "Box," **4**:61, *62*
Brown, H. Rap, **9**:142, 174
Brown, James, **9**:*175*, 176; **10**:89, 90, 92; **11**:22-23
Brown, John, **4**:30, 60; **5**:19
Brown v. *Board of Education* (1954), **7**:60; **8**:117; **9**:33-36, 66, 178; **10**:65
Brown, William Wells, **4**:111
Bruce, Blanche Kelso, **5**:*59*, 67; **6**:102, 103
Bryan, Andrew, **3**:94

Buffalo soldiers, **6**:30-31, 110
Bunche, Ralph, **8**:75, 79, 104; **9**:52, 155; **11**:23-24
Bunker Hill, Battle of, **3**:32
Burke, Clifford, **7**:150
Burke, Edmund, **3**:45-46
Burns, Anthony, **4**:120
Burroughs, Nannie Helen, **6**:132-33
Bush, George, **10**:87, 129-30
Bus boycotts, **9**:44-48, 49, 50-59, *62*, 64
Business owners, **6**:106-7, 108; **7**:19, 40, 75-78, 138-39, 148-49; **10**:60-63. *See also individual names*
Busing, school, **10**:65-67, *68*
Butler, Benjamin, **5**:25
Butler, Hilton, **8**:28-29
Butler, Octavia, **10**:104
Buttrick, Wallace, **7**:85
Butts, Calvin, **10**:96
Byrd, William, II, **2**:57

C

Cabeza de Vaca, Álvar Núñez, **2**:19-20
Cabral, Pedro Álvares, **1**:54
Calvin, John, **2**:29
Campbell, William, **2**:118-19
Capitalism, **10**:19-20
Cardozo, Francis L., **5**:46-47, 69
Caribbean immigration, **10**:7, 121-24
Caribbean islands
  British black troops in, **3**:49
  slave conditions, **2**:41
  slave population, **1**:11-12, 40, 43, 45, 109
  sugarcane industry, **1**:50-53; **2**:*43*; **3**:*18*
Carleton, Guy, **3**:49, 51
Carlos, John, **9**:*177*, 178
Carmichael, Stokely, **9**:139, *140*, 141-42, 174; **11**:24-25
Carr, Leroy, **8**:66
Carter, Jimmy, **10**:45

Carter, Robert, **3**:39, 67
Carter, Stephen L., **10**:56-58
Cartier, Jacques, **2**:24
Carver, George Washington, **6**:76, 86, 87-88; **11**:25-26
Catholic Church, **2**:18, 29, 42
Cayton, Horace R., **8**:21, 48, 79, 108
Certificates of freedom, **4**:*72*, 84, 85
Chaney, James, **9**:132-33
Charleston, South Carolina, **4**:94, 118, 130
Chaugham, James, **2**:105
Chavis, Benjamin, **10**:15-*16*
Cherokees, **4**:17
Chesnut, Mary Boykin, **4**:49-50
Chesnutt, Charles W., **6**:100, 116-18
Chicago, **7**:7, 77, *105*, 106-7, 108-9, 111, 112, 128-29; **10**:41, 81-83
Chicago Bee, **7**:77
Chicago Defender, **7**:91-92, 102, 106-7, 112, 129, 131, 145, 148
Chickasaws, **4**:17
Children. *See* Families
Chisholm, Shirley, **10**:33, *36-38*; **11**:26
Choctaws, **4**:17
Christianity, **2**:92-93
Christophe, Henri, **3**:127
Churches
  and civil rights movement, **9**:39, 46-48, 52-53, 86, 87
  in colonial America, **3**:66-67, 85-89, 93-96
  in early 20th century, **7**:19, 66-70, 125; **8**:67-68
  in late 19th century, **6**:13, 42, 79, 93-94, 95, 132-33
  and slavery, **4**:88-92; **5**:*102*, 131-34
  See also individual denominations
Cíbola, Seven Cities of, **2**:20

PICTURE CREDITS

◇ ◇ ◇

DAVID M. P. FREUND ◇ ◇ ◇

David M. P. Freund is a Ph.D. candidate in U.S. history at the University of Michigan. He writes about the politics of race and racism in 20th-century cities and suburbs. At the University of Michigan, he has coordinated instructor-training programs and conducted workshops on teaching writing in history courses. He received a Faculty Development grant to design curriculum materials for the undergraduate U.S. history survey.

MARYA ANNETTE McQUIRTER ◇ ◇ ◇

Marya Annette McQuirter is a Ph.D. candidate in history at the University of Michigan. Her dissertation is on black urban identity and leisure in the mid-20th century. She has presented papers at national and international symposia and is a contributor to *The Harvard Guide to African-American History.*

ROBIN D. G. KELLEY ◇ ◇ ◇

Robin D. G. Kelley is professor of history and Africana studies at New York University. He previously taught history and African-American studies at the University of Michigan. He is the author of *Hammer and Hoe: Alabama Communists during the Great Depression,* which received the Eliot Rudwick Prize of the Organization of American Historians and was named Outstanding Book on Human Rights by the Gustavus Myers Center for the Study of Human Rights in the United States. Professor Kelley is also the author of *Race Rebels: Culture, Politics, and the Black Working Class* and co-editor of *Imagining Home: Class, Culture, and Nationalism in the African Diaspora.*

EARL LEWIS ◇ ◇ ◇

Earl Lewis is professor of history and Afroamerican studies at the University of Michigan. He served as director of the university's Center for Afroamerican and African Studies from 1990 to 1993. Professor Lewis is the author of *In Their Own Interests: Race, Class and Power in Twentieth Century Norfolk* and co-author of *Blacks in the Industrial Age: A Documentary History.*